adaiyalam

AKSHEYAA AKILAN

INDIA • SINGAPORE • MALAYSIA

ISBN
Hardcase 979-8-89961-812-3
Paperback 979-8-89906-935-2

Contents

Prelude: The Invisible Chains

I'm Aksheyaa—a mental health professional, and social entrepreneur passionate about reshaping the way we understand mental health, neurodivergence, and healing. My work sits at the intersection of mental health, gender justice, and systemic reform. It is driven by a deep commitment to making care more accessible, inclusive, and culturally grounded.

But this journey wasn't just a career choice—it was a personal reckoning.

I have spent years searching for a sense of home within myself. Like many of us, I grew up believing that identity was something given to me rather than something I could define. I was told– who I should be, how I should speak, what I should value, and what success should look like. I was taught to admire the polished, the Western, the modern, to question the worth of the indigenous, the intuitive, the ancestral. Without realizing it, I absorbed these lessons, internalizing the idea that to be successful, to be valid, I had to shed parts of myself.

I founded Hibiscus Foundation for Social Welfare, Hibiscus Counselling, and Hibiscus Connect, building community-driven support systems that have impacted over 100,000 people. Through these initiatives, I provide mental health services, legal aid, and economic empowerment— particularly for survivors of gender-based violence and individuals without financial independence. My goal is to challenge the colonial, patriarchal, and caste-based barriers that continue to shape mental health care and access today.

My journey in this field is deeply personal. Living with **depression, ADHD, dyslexia, and dyscalculia**, I've had to navigate a world that wasn't built for minds like mine. These experiences shaped my understanding of neurodivergence, systemic oppression, and the need for decolonized mental health care—one that honors collective healing, indigenous wisdom, and intersectionality.

This book is an exploration of what it means to decolonize **not just institutions, but our minds, our relationships, and our very sense of self.** It is about dismantling the binaries that keep us trapped— modern versus traditional, Western versus indigenous, rational versus emotional—and embracing the complexity of who we are.

What happens when the version of success we chase is rooted in systems that were never meant for us? When our worth is measured against standards designed to keep us striving but never arriving? The deeper I delved into my work in mental health, human rights, and social change, the more I saw how colonial legacies shape everything—from our education to our beauty standards, from our healthcare to our self-worth. I began to notice the quiet ways I had been conditioned to see myself through someone else's lens. And I realized that if I wanted to reclaim my identity, I had to start with unlearning, personally.

This book is deeply personal, but it is also grounded in history. As a Tamil woman, my heritage is steeped in a legacy of resistance, self-sufficiency, and knowledge systems that predate colonial rule. Tamil Nadu has a rich history of philosophy, literature, and healing practices that thrived before European intervention. Yet, much of this wisdom has been erased, dismissed, or co-opted by colonial frameworks that prioritize Western knowledge while disregarding indigenous ways of knowing.

The very word *Adaiyalam*—a Tamil term meaning identity, mark, or sign—embodies the essence of this book. It is about reclaiming what was lost, restoring what was stolen, and reimagining a future that honors our past. Tamil history, from the Sangam era to present-day struggles for linguistic and cultural preservation, forms the backbone of this exploration. This is not just a theoretical discussion; it is an invitation to remember and reclaim.

75 Years of Independence, Yet...

India has been independent for **75 years**, so why am I talking to you about colonization? What does it have to do with us now?

On the surface, we are no longer colonized. The British left, our land is ours, and governance is in our hands. But is that all colonization ever was? A foreign power ruling over us?

If you ask me, colonization isn't just about **land and borders**—it's about **control over our minds, values, and identities**. While political colonization ended, its invisible roots remained deeply embedded in our culture, shaping how we define beauty, intelligence, success, and even healing.

This book will introduce two constructs:

Social Colonization – The way colonial ideals continue to shape our **social structures, institutions, and power dynamics**.

Cultural Colonization – The way our **languages, traditions, and ways of knowing** have been replaced or devalued in favor of Western standards.

Through history, storytelling, and critical analysis, I'll explore how **globalization, media, and education have sustained these colonial ideologies**—often in ways we don't even recognize.

Beyond my work in therapy and advocacy, I've contributed to **Tamil Nadu State Human Rights Commission, United Nations human rights initiatives and the World Health Organization**, pushing for policy-level change in mental health and disability rights. As a **WHO FIDES Health Influencer**, I use my voice to amplify conversations around mental health, gender-based violence, and neurodivergence—both in global policy spaces and at the grassroots level.

But this book is not just about institutions. It's about **you, me, and the quiet, insidious ways we still carry the weight of a history we did not choose.** This book has images of my kith and kin through the years and narrations about my experience and my history to draw parallel to what once was.

My journey has been one of contradictions—**between the expectations placed upon me and the truths I have come to embrace, between what I was told I should be and what I am becoming.** This book is for anyone who has felt that conflict, who has questioned their place in a world that seems determined to shape them in its image. It is for those who are ready to reclaim their narrative.

Unlearning is not easy, and reclaiming is not always comfortable. But it is necessary.

And it begins here.

Chapter 1

Illusion of Freedom: The Inherited Cage

"இக்கரைக்கு அக்கறை பச்சை"
"The grass is greener on the other side."

Or, is it?
I was taught to speak in a language that was not my own,
to shape my thoughts in borrowed frames.
They told me stories where my people were missing,
their voices replaced, their echoes erased.

They mapped the world in lines I did not draw,
taught me to walk a path I did not choose.
History came wrapped in borrowed syllables,
and I was told to find myself in its shadows.

But my name is carved into earth and wind,
not in the ink of conquerors' pens.
My roots remember what my mind forgot—
that I am not lost.
I was displaced.

So I gather the pieces, the words, the ways,
I stitch myself back into the fabric of knowing.

Not just for me, but for all who were told
that their truth was too wild, too broken, too much.

This is my mark.
My Adaiyalam.
Not given—
but reclaimed.

Colonialism—a chapter in history books. A story of invasions, resistance, and independence movements. A wound we were told had begun to heal.

But colonialism was never just about land.

It was about power. The power to dictate what is normal, what is beautiful, what is civilized. And that power still lingers—in the way we think, speak, dress, and even see ourselves.

Decolonization isn't just an intellectual pursuit for me. It is deeply personal.

It's in the way I've had to fight to see my own reflection as beautiful. In the way I've had to unlearn the discomfort I once felt wearing my own cultural attire. In the way I still catch myself switching languages to be taken more seriously.

I grew up in a world that told me, in subtle and not-so-subtle ways, that my dusky skin was not beautiful. That fairness was the aspiration. But that wasn't always the case.

Before colonization, beauty in India was shaped by caste, power, and privilege—just as it is today. The standards were different, but exclusion was the constant. Colonial rule didn't create colorism, but it weaponized it, making proximity to whiteness the new ideal.

The obsession with fairness that lingers today isn't just a colonial hangover—it's a symptom of deeper hierarchies that have always existed. And yet, somewhere along the way, we started believing otherwise.

It's in the language I speak so effortlessly:the English words that roll off my tongue as if they have always belonged to me. But they didn't. English was imposed, made necessary, while my mother tongue—our languages—were pushed to the margins, deemed lesser, informal, uncultured. The way I structure my thoughts, the phrases I default to, even the way I write this book—traces of colonialism linger in every word.

It's in the clothes we wear. Why does a sari feel like a statement while a suit feels like neutrality? Why does wearing pants or a shirt feel like it's modern? "Why is wearing a saree seen as an act of tradition, a cultural statement, or even a political act—rather than just clothing, just being?" Why do we measure professionalism through the lens of the colonizer, in Western ideals of formality and structure?

I started noticing these fractures in my own life. In the way education rewarded a particular way of thinking—one that didn't account for neurodivergence.

In the way therapy, meant to heal, often alienated those who didn't fit into its Eurocentric definitions of mental health. Some notable contemporary models are (like culturally adapted cognitive-behavioral therapy) emerging to address these gaps but not without resistance. There's a long way to go. Similarly, in the way medicine dismissed centuries of indigenous knowledge, only to repackage and rebrand it later.

Tamil history is one of resilience, knowledge, and continuous reinvention. From the Sangam era's flourishing literary and trade networks to the Chola dynasty's naval dominance, Tamil civilization has long been a center of art, philosophy, and governance. The Tamil language, one of the oldest surviving classical languages, carries within it millennia of poetry, resistance, and identity.

Colonial rule disrupted this continuum, imposing new hierarchies and erasing indigenous ways of being—but Tamil identity endured. From the anti-colonial uprisings of the Marudhu Brothers to the Dravidian movement's assertion of self-respect and linguistic pride, Tamil history has been a constant struggle against erasure, an ongoing act of reclamation. Today, decolonization in a Tamil context means remembering that our heritage was never static—it was always evolving, resisting, and redefining itself on its own terms.

That's when I understood: colonialism didn't just shape the borders of countries. It shaped the borders of our minds. It dictated how we think, how we heal, how we define ourselves. And decolonization isn't just about reclaiming land—it's about reclaiming our ways of knowing, feeling, and existing.

The impact of colonisation was neither uniform nor equal—its fractures ran differently through rural and urban India. In urban centers, colonisation ushered in a wave of Western education, administrative restructuring, and industrialization. English became the language of power, and a new class of anglicized elites emerged—often alienated from indigenous knowledge systems. Cities became the testing ground for colonial policies and the performance of modernity.

In contrast, rural areas experienced a different wound: land revenue systems like the Zamindari and Ryotwari gutted local agrarian economies, fractured communal land ownership, and deepened caste-based oppression. Rural livelihoods became more precarious as indigenous practices were criminalized or replaced, while urban aspirations became modeled on colonial values of civility and success. The unevenness persists today—where cities carry the illusion of progress, villages often bear the burden of erasure.

As I write this, I feel the weight of generations pressing down on me. The anger sits in my chest, tight and unrelenting—not just for myself, but for everyone who has been made to shrink, to conform, to erase themselves just to exist in a world that was never built for them. It's the anger of realizing that my thoughts, my language, even the way I see my own body, have been shaped by something insidious, something I never consented to.

And beneath that anger is grief—grief for the parts of us that were stolen, for the voices that were silenced, for the traditions that were branded as primitive while others took and profited from them. The sadness of knowing that even as I fight to unlearn, the remnants of colonialism are so deeply embedded that they feel like home. But they are not home. And maybe that's why this hurts so much. Because to decolonize is to mourn what was lost while still daring to reclaim what's left.

Decolonization matters to me because I know what it's like to be disconnected from myself. To believe, even unconsciously, that whiteness is the standard. That Western medicine is the only valid form of healing. That my own way of thinking—shaped by neurodivergence—was a flaw rather than a different kind of intelligence.

It matters because I've been in rooms where conventional therapy and medical systems failed people like me, not because healing wasn't possible, but because the framework itself wasn't built for us. Because I know what it's like to search for belonging in a system that was never designed for people like me to belong.

Decolonization is important to me because I want to reclaim what was taken—not just for myself, but for everyone who has ever felt that rupture between who they are and who they were taught they should be.

Because I refuse to spend my life conforming to an illusion when I could be dismantling it instead.

A little story: Tales will glorify the hunter until the Lion learns to write

*The classroom smelled of chalk dust and old wood, the air thick with the weight of unspoken rules. **Ananya** sat at the front, back straight, fingers clenched around her pencil. The teacher had just finished explaining the assignment: Write a short essay about an important historical figure.*

"Can I write about Velu Nachiyar?" Ananya asked hesitantly.

The teacher's lips pursed. "It's best to choose someone with more global recognition—like Churchill, Gandhi, or Lincoln."

Ananya swallowed the protest rising in her throat. Velu Nachiyar had been the first queen in India to fight the British, strategizing against them long before 1857. But here, in this English-medium school, history meant something different. It meant battles won by those who had written the textbooks.

At lunchtime, she found her grandfather in the courtyard, waiting to walk her home. His wrinkled hands held her school bag like it was something precious.

"Tatha," she asked, as they walked past the bakery where the smell of warm puffs and tea filled the street. "Why don't they teach us about our history?"

Her grandfather stopped, looking at her with eyes that had seen too much. "Because history is not just what happened, ma. It's also who gets to tell the story."

That evening, Ananya sat at her desk, staring at the blank paper in front of her. Then, with steady hands, she began to write. Not about Churchill. Not about Lincoln. But about Velu Nachiyar—the queen who had set fire to an armory before anyone thought rebellion was possible.

And when the school bell rang the next morning, she walked in with her essay, her voice steady, her history intact.

This book is about reclamation. It is an invitation to unlearn, to question, to deconstruct the invisible forces that shape our thoughts, our relationships, our bodies, and our futures. It is about finding new ways—or rather, remembering old ways—to exist in the world.

Once we begin to see them, we cannot unsee them. And that is where the work begins. This is not just about understanding history; it is about unlearning the ways it continues to shape us. It is about questioning the definitions we have inherited—of beauty, intelligence, professionalism, even healing—and asking who created them and why. It is about mourning what was lost while daring to reclaim what remains.

While reclaiming indigenous and pre-colonial practices, it is essential to acknowledge that not everything from the past was just or equitable. Many societies had draconian traditions—some rooted in caste, gender discrimination, or rigid social hierarchies—that should not be romanticized or carried forward. However, the existence of harmful practices does not invalidate the wisdom, balance, and interdependence that many of our ancestral traditions upheld. Decolonization is not about blindly reviving the past but about discerning what serves us, what heals us, and what allows us to build relationships rooted in justice, respect, and cultural authenticity.

Decolonization is a process, a rupture, a return. And perhaps most importantly, it is an act of liberation—not just for ourselves, but for those who will come after us.

My aunt, Sudha and her classmates performing Karakattam in 1980s (Karakattam is a vibrant, traditional Tamil folk dance from Tamil Nadu, India, performed as a tribute to the rain goddess Mariamman, often during temple festivals and celebrations, and characterized by dancers balancing a decorated pot (karakam) on their heads while performing.)

At the end of each chapter, I leave you with questions—not for passive reflection, but for active deconstruction. Sit with them. Wrestle with them. Let them challenge you:

When did you first learn what "beauty" is supposed to look like? Who defined it for you?

Do you think in the language of your ancestors or the language of your colonizers?

What does "professionalism" mean to you? Who decided that definition?

If you had never seen a map, how would you describe the world?

Have you ever dismissed knowledge because it wasn't written in a textbook?

Whose voices have shaped your beliefs the most? Are they truly yours?

Chapter 2

Unlearning the Lies: Intelligence, Success, and Self-Worth

"கற்றது கைமண் அளவு , கல்லாதது உலகளவு"
"What one knows is only a handful, whereas the unknown is the size of the world."

They told me intelligence was a straight line—
neatly written, sharply spoken, measured in scores.
But my mind didn't move in straight lines.
It jumped, skipped, found meaning in the spaces between.

They told me I was slow, that I struggled,
but I was only reading differently—
seeing the whole before the parts,
grasping the rhythm before the letters.

I was taught that success had a language,
and it was not mine.
My colonisers tongue, crisp and polished, was the only currency,
while my mother tongue sat quietly in the corner,
waiting for permission to exist.

Self-worth came in checkboxes—
Degrees. Titles. Productivity.
Rest was indulgence.
Doubt was weakness.
Burnout was the price of belonging.

But tell me—
What is intelligence if not the wisdom of my ancestors,
who read the stars like scripture?
What is success if not the hands that heal,
the voices that carry history,
the art that survives empires?

I am done chasing worth
through borrowed definitions.
I am learning to see myself
not as they wrote me,
but as I was always meant to be.

As a child, I was told that intelligence meant excelling in math and science, thinking in straight lines, and being able to produce quick, logical answers.

It took me years to realize that intelligence could also look like storytelling, emotional intuition, and nonlinear thinking—things that were never rewarded in school. But why do we define intelligence so narrowly? Who decided what it should look like?

By every conventional measure of success, I should be the ideal. I hold five degrees in Psychology and Human Rights, multiple titles including being a Social Entrepreneur and Mental Health Professional, and have built organizations from the ground up. My productivity levels are far beyond the average—if hours of work were the only metric, I would be considered exceptional. I have spoken on global stages, been recognized by institutions that define excellence, and have the credentials that society deems valuable.

And yet, none of it was ever enough.

Because success, as we know it, was never designed to be fulfilling—it was designed to be a moving target, always just out of reach. It was built on systems that thrive on inadequacy, on the belief that no matter how much we achieve, we must keep striving for more. More wealth, more status, more validation—each milestone only shifting the goalpost further.

True fulfillment was never part of the equation; instead, we are conditioned to chase an illusion, mistaking exhaustion for progress and external validation for self-worth. To break free, we must redefine success on our own terms—grounded in purpose, contentment, and a sense of wholeness that is not dictated by systems designed to keep us running.

The Colonial Framework of Intelligence

The Western world has long equated intelligence with linguistic and mathematical ability—skills reinforced within their own societies. But what of the farmer who knows the rhythms of the land? The artisan who weaves stories into fabric? The healer who understands the body beyond clinical diagnostics? Are they not intelligent? Or have we simply failed to value their knowledge?

The dominant definition of intelligence, shaped largely by colonial frameworks, prioritizes:

Logical-Analytical Thinking – Intelligence is equated with linear, rational problem-solving.

Academic Achievement – Intelligence is linked to excelling in formal education and standardized testing.

Linguistic Proficiency – Fluency in English and dominant European languages is seen as a marker of intelligence, while indigenous languages are disregarded.

Individual Problem-Solving – Intelligence is associated with independent thinking rather than collective wisdom.

Technological and Scientific Mastery – Innovation in STEM fields is celebrated, while emotional and artistic intelligence remain undervalued.

Productivity and Efficiency – Intelligence is measured by output and speed, rather than depth of understanding or lived experience.

This narrow view ignores the richness of intelligence found in indigenous knowledge systems, emotional depth, creativity, and communal wisdom.

Shift in Knowledge Systems

Before colonization, learning was deeply integrated into daily life. Knowledge was significantly passed down through oral traditions, storytelling, and practical applications.

In Tamil society, education was never confined to classrooms or written texts—it was a lived experience, passed down through generations in ways that nurtured both intellect and intuition. The Tamil Sangam era (circa 300 BCE – 300 CE) saw poets, philosophers, and scholars engage in literary and scientific discussions, where knowledge was woven into poetry, astronomy, medicine, and ethics.

Gurukuls and temple schools taught not just scriptures but also mathematics, astronomy, and indigenous healing practices, often tailored to a student's natural inclinations. Palm-leaf manuscripts preserved scientific and philosophical knowledge, while folk traditions carried wisdom through song and storytelling. Intelligence was never measured in isolation but seen as part of one's contribution to society—whether through craftsmanship, healing, or governance.

Note: *While Gurukuls and temple schools once nurtured holistic learning—from mathematics to astronomy and healing—access was deeply restricted by caste, and this legacy of exclusion is one we must consciously dismantle, not carry forward into modern mental health or education spaces.*

The idea that learning had to be compartmentalized into rigid subjects or assessed through standardized tests was an alien concept, introduced much later through colonial frameworks that sought to replace holistic education with rote learning.

British colonization reshaped this. Thomas Macaulay, in his infamous *Minute on Indian Education* (1835), dismissed indigenous knowledge systems as worthless, advocating for an English-based education that would create a class of Indians who were, in his words, *"Indian in blood and colour, but English in tastes, in opinions, in morals, and in intellect."* However, while Macaulay played a key role, Indian education systems were already shifting under earlier colonial interventions. It wasn't a singular moment but a gradual restructuring.

Generations later, we still live under this shadow.

Indigenous knowledge systems valued holistic thinking, intuition, and community wisdom. In India, institutions like Nalanda and Takshashila existed long before British rule and had structured curricula. Islamic madrasas and gurukuls also had rigorous education systems, though they were different from Western models.

Yet, colonial education dismissed these as unscientific, forcing people to measure their intelligence against a framework that was never meant for them. Learning was no longer an interconnected, communal process but an isolated intellectual pursuit based on rote memorization and standardized assessment.

When intelligence is framed in such rigid terms, self-worth becomes deeply entangled with fitting into this mold. Entire cultures and knowledge systems have been marginalized because they do not conform to an imposed hierarchy, leaving generations questioning their own brilliance simply because their ways of knowing were never considered valid.

The consequences of this imposed hierarchy were far-reaching. If intelligence was defined by colonial standards, then self-worth became tied to fitting within that model. Success meant excelling in school, mastering English, and adopting Western frameworks of thought.

The Cost of Conformity

For many of us, this legacy lingers.

The shame of struggling with rote memorization when our ancestors learned through storytelling. The anxiety of speaking our mother tongue in professional spaces, fearing it makes us sound less competent. The quiet insecurity of feeling "less intelligent" because our ways of learning, thinking, and existing do not fit within colonial structures.

The pressure to be "rational," to argue in a way that mirrors European philosophies, and to navigate the world through individualistic achievement leaves little room for alternative ways of knowing. Those who struggle within these systems—not because they lack intelligence, but because they process and understand the world differently—are made to feel inadequate.

But intelligence was never meant to be confined to a single definition. It is fluid, dynamic, and deeply cultural. Reclaiming our self-worth means challenging the narrow lens through which we were taught to see ourselves—understanding that intelligence is not just logic and language but wisdom, connection, and lived experience.

And yet, we have adapted. We learned to speak the language of institutions, to master the tools of a world that was not built with us in mind. We have picked up the mantle, not just to survive but to excel. We carry within us both the knowledge of our ancestors and the realities of a globalized world.

But adaptation does not mean surrender. It is not too late to unlearn the belief that our worth is measured only by how well we fit into these systems. It is not too late to expand what success, intelligence, and progress can mean. We are still evolving, still rediscovering the richness of ways we were once made to forget. And in doing so, we are shaping something new—where both the wisdom of the past and the possibilities of the future can coexist.

Decolonizing Success and Worth

Colonialism didn't just redefine intelligence—it restructured human worth itself. Colonizers needed labor to fuel their empires, and capitalism ensured that labor became the defining measure of a person's value. Productivity became the currency of worth, and those who couldn't "contribute" to the economy in profitable ways were seen as lesser. The colonized, the caregivers, the artisans—those whose work didn't translate into direct wealth for the powerful—were dehumanized, their roles diminished.

We've inherited this belief system without question. Even today, being "useful" is synonymous with being productive. Rest feels indulgent. Slowness feels lazy. The guilt of not constantly achieving something gnaws at us, a byproduct of generations conditioned to believe that time is money and idleness is waste. We wear exhaustion like a badge of honor, equating overwork with success, unable to sit still without feeling like we're falling behind.

And yet, not all labor is valued equally. The jobs that sustain communities—teaching, caregiving, healing, creating—are often the least respected. Meanwhile, those that extract, exploit, and accumulate wealth are glorified. Colonialism and capitalism framed labor not in terms of its contribution to humanity but in terms of its profitability.

So, we must ask ourselves:
Who benefits from our burnout?
Why do we feel guilty for resting?
And most importantly, how do we begin to untangle our worth from our work?

One evening, as Rajkumar (my husband) and I sat together after dinner, I asked him a question that had been on my mind.

Me: *What would you do if our future kids wanted to go abroad to study and work?*

He paused for a moment before answering.

Rajkumar: *I'd be sad that they're not near me, but if that's what they want, I would support them.*

His response was expected, yet something about it made me push further.

Me: *Wouldn't you want them to be successful? To achieve more?*

He tilted his head slightly.

Rajkumar: *Successful how?*

Me: *You know, getting into big universities, making a name for themselves, earning well.*

He looked at me, thoughtful, before asking a question that completely disarmed me.

Rajkumar: *What if that's not what they think success is?*

I blinked.

Rajkumar: *What if success to them means being comfortable? Being close to home? Having the privilege of visiting family whenever they'd like?*

I had no response. I just sat there, staring at him, as I felt my own perception of success begin to unravel.

How much of what I believed was truly mine? And how much had been taught to me?

Language as a Colonial Tool

Language was never just a tool of communication under colonial rule—it was a weapon. English became the dominant language not just through policy but through power, used to separate the "civilized" from the "uncivilized," the educated from the uneducated, the worthy from the unworthy. Even today, accents and grammar dictate perceptions of competence, and those who struggle with English—especially in former colonies—are dismissed as less intelligent, no matter how profound their knowledge may be in their own language.

Education systems still reflect this colonial legacy. Western philosophers, scientists, and thinkers dominate school curricula, their ideas presented as the foundation of human knowledge.

The education system introduced by our colonizers was never meant to empower—it was designed to create obedient workers, not independent thinkers. Under British rule, traditional Indian education, which once thrived in gurukuls, madrasas, and local learning systems, was dismantled and replaced with a rigid, standardized curriculum.

The goal was not to nurture creativity, critical thinking, or indigenous knowledge but to mass-produce clerks and bureaucrats who could serve the colonial administration without questioning its authority. By enforcing English as the primary medium of instruction and prioritizing British literature, law, and history, they ensured that generations of Indians would internalize Western superiority while disconnecting from their own heritage.

Schools became factories, churning out laborers for the British economy—people who could read and write just enough to follow orders but never enough to challenge the systems that controlled them. Even today, the remnants of this colonial model persist, conditioning us to prioritize rote memorization over innovation, compliance over curiosity, and validation from external authorities over self-directed learning.

We are taught about Descartes, but not about the deep philosophical traditions of Africa or Asia. We celebrate Newton, but indigenous knowledge of astronomy, medicine, and mathematics—developed centuries before—remains absent. The result? A belief that all important discoveries came from Europe, as if the rest of the world contributed nothing.

History is no different. In textbooks, colonizers become explorers, invaders become heroes, and resistance movements are reduced to footnotes. The violence of the empire is softened, its crimes justified under the guise of "progress."

A short story: Faking fevers, praying for floods:

Aadi: What happened to you? You look like you just ran a marathon.

Ravi: I wish. At least then I'd have a reason to be this drained. It's just… school, man. I can't do it anymore.

Aadi: I feel you. I spent the first ten minutes of the morning praying for a flood. Full monsoon manifestation.

Ravi: Bro, I literally googled "how to fake a fever" last night. Almost burned my forehead with a hot spoon just to get out of today's test.

Aadi: And this is what they call "the best years of our lives."

Ravi: Yeah, if you enjoy memorizing a bunch of nonsense, spitting it out on an answer sheet, and forgetting it immediately after.

Aadi: The only thing school has actually taught me is how to survive extreme pressure with minimal sleep.

Ravi: And how to write absolute crap in an exam that *sounds* smart but says nothing.

Aadi: Honestly, half of us are just figuring out the best way to play the system. Nobody cares about actually learning. It's just about getting through.

Ravi: And it's wild because I *like* learning! I just don't like whatever *this* is.

Aadi: Exactly! If school was actually about learning, we'd be out doing things, asking real questions, experimenting. Not getting penalized for writing an answer in our own words instead of the exact phrasing from the textbook.

Ravi: It's a joke. And the worst part? If you can't keep up, the system just discards you. Like, "Oh, you're struggling? Too bad. Work harder." No one stops to ask if maybe the system itself is the problem.

Aadi: And the teachers aren't even the villains here! They're stuck in this too, following the same broken rules.

Ravi: So what do we do? Keep faking fevers and hoping for floods?

Aadi: Or we figure out how to actually learn beyond this nonsense.

Ravi: You mean… like an education rebellion?

Aadi: I mean… What do we have to lose?

Modern productivity culture is often critiqued through the lens of capitalism, but it's equally vital to examine how both colonialism and caste shaped our relationship with work and worth. While many indigenous and pre-colonial societies in South Asia had sustainable rhythms of labor, rest, and communal contribution rooted in cultural values, these systems were also marked by deeply entrenched caste hierarchies that dictated who could work, rest, or lead. Colonialism intensified this injustice—not only by exploiting labor but by reinforcing caste-based divisions, introducing rigid time discipline, and embedding extractive, output-driven models of productivity that continue to value efficiency over dignity and collective well-being.

While critiquing these colonial impositions, it is also important to recognize that knowledge exchange between cultures predates colonialism. Trade, migration, and intellectual dialogue have long shaped how different societies understand work and progress. The challenge, then, is not to reject productivity altogether but to reclaim and reimagine it in ways that prioritize sustainability, collective well-being, and cultural relevance.

Reclaiming productivity is not about rejecting ambition or efficiency—it is about redefining them on our own terms. It is about severing the grip of colonial values that equate worth with exhaustion and returning to ways of working that honor balance, rest, and collective well-being.

We do not have to measure our days in billable hours or our lives in economic output. Instead, we can draw from the wisdom of cultures that thrived before the clock became a master, before profit eclipsed purpose. Productivity does not have to be a tool of oppression; it can be a force for liberation. The question is not whether we will work—it is how, for whom, and toward what future.

Questions to sit with and reflect

How has the pressure to conform to colonial ways of thinking shaped the way you see your own intelligence?

In what ways have you adapted to fit into these systems, and what parts of yourself did you have to leave behind in the process?

What aspects of knowledge, learning, or wisdom from your own culture feel undervalued in mainstream spaces?

How can you begin to unlearn the idea that intelligence must look a certain way?

What would it mean to reclaim your own way of knowing, thinking, and being—without apology?

If we could redefine success on our own terms, what would it look like for you?

How do we balance the skills we've gained through adaptation with a return to more authentic, indigenous, or intuitive ways of being?

What does it mean to truly honor the knowledge of our ancestors while living in the modern world?

My mother, Anandhi Akilan and her classmates in 1980

Chapter 3

Gender Before Erasure: We Were Always More

பொய் உடை ஒருவன் சொல் வன்மையினால்
மெய்போலும்மே மெய்போலும்மே.
The falsehood of a liar by reason of its force, may appear like truth, may appear like truth.

Adaiyalam – A Name for Who We Were

They taught us to shrink,
to fit within boxes drawn in foreign ink,
to stand straight, speak soft,
be man, be woman—be nothing else.

But before their lines,
before their rules,
we were endless.

We were the ones who walked between worlds,
who wove our names into the wind,
who danced beyond the weight of words,
who held no shame in the way we adorned our skin,
our bodies, our love, our lives.

And then came the erasure.
The rulers, the laws, the whispers—
cutting us down into two clean halves,
leaving no space for the in-between,
for the shifting, the sacred, the true.

But we are *not* made of silence.
We are the echoes of a time before cages,
the hands that remember how to break them.

They taught us to shrink.
We taught us to unlearn,
and we relearn.
We *choose* to take up space.

Sangam poetry, particularly in texts like the *Kuruntokai* and *Akananuru*, celebrated beauty in a way that reflected Tamil geography and lifestyles. Dark skin, adorned with fragrant oils and turmeric, was praised as resplendent. Women were described as having "black-streaked hair scented with flowers," "skin dark as rain-filled clouds," and eyes "wide as the ocean." Beauty was not confined to a singular complexion but was described in ways that highlighted the richness of nature—whether dusky like fertile soil or golden like a ripened harvest.

Tamil literature also rejected passive, delicate ideals of beauty. Women were often portrayed as strong and self-assured, with beauty interwoven with their wisdom, resilience, and participation in daily life. Female warriors (*Veerangai*), merchants, poets, and rulers existed alongside the romanticized imagery of lovers and nurturers. There was no contradiction in a woman being both beautiful and powerful.

The Gender Binary as a Colonial Construct

For centuries, pre-colonial societies across the world recognized gender beyond the rigid male-female binary. Hijras in South Asia held sacred roles, Two-Spirit people in Indigenous North American cultures were honored as carriers of both masculine and feminine spirits, and Fa'afafine in Samoa moved fluidly through gender roles without question.

Gender was not simply biology—it was cultural, spiritual, and diverse.

Then came colonialism. With it arrived a rigid binary that framed anything outside of "man" and "woman" as unnatural, immoral, and, eventually, illegal. The imposition of Western legal, religious, and educational systems erased gender diversity, criminalized queerness, and embedded shame in those who did not conform. This colonial framework did not just define who could be a "man" or a "woman," but also dictated how those roles should be performed, suppressing centuries of fluid gender expressions and practices.

Tamil texts, temple sculptures, and folk traditions suggest a more fluid understanding of gender than the binary later imposed by Victorian morality. The deity Ardhanarishvara—Shiva in an androgynous form, half-male and half-female—symbolized the idea that masculinity and femininity were not rigid but complementary forces within every being.

Additionally, Tamil folklore and temple inscriptions reference *Panar* and *Kudisai Nayanmar*—performers, mystics, and ascetics who often occupied gender-fluid roles. Some were revered for embodying both masculine and feminine energies, and their identities were socially accepted rather than erased or criminalized.

The colonial encounter altered these perspectives. British rule imposed Victorian gender norms, where masculinity became linked to rationality and authority, while femininity was redefined through submissiveness and domesticity. The colonizers also introduced colorism, where fairness became associated with superiority—a contrast to the pre-colonial admiration for darker skin tones.

By reconstructing beauty and gender through European frameworks, colonial rule disrupted centuries of Tamil cultural expressions, replacing them with shame, rigid binaries, and Western standards that persist even today. Reclaiming these indigenous ideals requires re-examining Tamil texts, oral traditions, and artistic expressions that once honored diversity in form, gender, and beauty.

Gender Roles and Their Colonial Roots

What we often accept as "traditional" gender roles are, in many ways, not as ancient as we think. While pre-colonial societies across the world—including in South Asia—had diverse and complex understandings of gender, colonial rule brought with it rigid binaries and patriarchal norms that rewrote social structures. This is something that impacts everyone till date, personally.

I was born a girl. That alone came with consequences.

I am the first woman in my paternal family to earn a college degree. But that fact does not erase the weight I was born with—the burden of being a daughter in Dharmapuri, a district notorious for female foeticide and infanticide. I had a loving family and yet, I was raised with the echo of a hundred whispered warnings: Girls are burdens.

Women must adjust. Compromise. Endure. A woman is to blame if she does not bear a son. A woman must dress modestly, must not laugh too loudly, must sit properly, must never demand too much space.

Men, too, carry their own chains. A man must never cry. He must never cook, never clean, never care too much,—those are tasks beneath him.

He must earn for his family, he must be strong, must be respected, and must provide.

But this was not always our truth.

Once, women walked in sarees without blouses, unashamed of their bodies, unburdened by the colonial gaze that would later sexualize and police them.

A photo of my Grandmother-in-law and her sister and their husband. The women had "pachakutu" (tattooed bodies) and they never wore blouses.

Once, women worked in the fields alongside men, carrying their newborns with them, laboring not as secondary beings but as equals.

Once, gender roles were not dictated by colonial scripts of "proper femininity" and "respectable masculinity," but by the needs of the community, by the flow of life itself.

Before colonization, Tamil society held a far more fluid and expansive understanding of gender and beauty than the rigid norms introduced by colonial rule. The Tamil Sangam era (circa 300 BCE – 300 CE) offers rich literary evidence that beauty was deeply tied to one's connection with nature, virtue, and personal expression rather than strict Eurocentric ideals of fairness or fragility.

Reclaiming Interdependence

Hyper-independence is often survival—it is the response to a world that has denied autonomy, especially to women and marginalized genders. We have had to be independent to break out of patriarchal control, to carve spaces where we are not just someone's daughter, wife, or mother. But in that struggle, we must also remember where we once stood. Before colonialism imposed rigid gender roles, before capitalism demanded individual success, we lived in collectivistic societies where dependence was not weakness but a shared responsibility. Communities raised children together, labor was divided based on skill and need rather than gendered restrictions, and support was woven into the fabric of daily life. The solution is not to swing from forced dependence to relentless independence, but to reclaim interdependence—where we can lean on each other without losing ourselves, where strength is found in connection, not just in standing alone. True liberation is not just the ability to walk away from oppressive systems but also the freedom to embrace support without shame.

Gender and the Body: Colorism, Clothing, and Beauty Standards

Colonialism not only dictated how we should act, but how we should look. Fair skin became currency; a standard of beauty imposed by those who saw darkness as inferiority. Eurocentric features were elevated, while our own were erased, diminished, or altered through skin-lightening creams, plastic surgery, and chemical straighteners.

Modesty, too, was rewritten under colonial rule. The saree, once worn with ease and practicality, became a site of shame—women were forced to cover up, to present themselves as "civilized," as "respectable." Clothing, skin, hair, and laughter all became battlegrounds where we were forced to prove our worth within the narrow confines of colonial morality.

Caste-specific beauty standards in South Asia were deeply entrenched long before colonial rule, rooted in Brahmanical patriarchy, which upheld fairness, specific facial features, and body types as markers of purity and caste superiority.

Dalit feminist scholars like Sharmila Rege and Yashica Dutt have argued that these beauty hierarchies not only dictated desirability but also access to dignity, marriage, and social mobility. In *Coming Out as Dalit*, Dutt discusses how these beauty standards continue to shape self-perception and societal acceptance, with fair skin and upper-caste aesthetics still dominating mainstream media and matrimonial preferences. To challenge this, a decolonial and anti-caste feminist lens must recognize that casteism in beauty is not merely a colonial import but a historically persistent form of exclusion that has evolved through different eras of oppression.

The Intersection of Gender and Capitalism

The colonial project did not end with legal and social control—it seeped into economic structures as well. The division of labor by gender—men as breadwinners, women as caregivers—was not simply an organic evolution but an imposed system designed to serve capital. Women's unpaid labor became the backbone of households, while men's work was valued and compensated.

Even today, we see the remnants of this in pink-collar jobs, in the expectation that women will do emotional labor, in the glorification of "empowered" women who succeed within a system that was never built for them. Real systemic change does not lie in the illusion of empowerment through corporate feminism, but in dismantling the very structures that exploit labor along gendered lines.

Reclaiming Gender: What It Truly Means to Be Who You Are

To decolonize gender is to return to a space of freedom—where our identities are not dictated by the remnants of a system that was never meant to serve us. It is to remember that gender was never meant to be confined. It is to embrace fluidity, to honor histories that were erased, and to reclaim the right to exist as we truly are, beyond binaries, beyond expectations, beyond the echoes of colonial rule.

My journey as a woman has been shaped by these histories, by these contradictions, by the push and pull of inherited beliefs and decolonial truths. I have had to unlearn the shame, the silence, the fear. I have had to reclaim space where I was told I did not belong.

And I know this is only the beginning.

> *"Why is there a rule for everything?" Meera asked, kicking at the pebbles on the school steps.*

Arjun looked up from his half-eaten snack. "What do you mean?"

She sighed. "I mean…for being a girl. For being a boy. For just existing. There's a rule for how I should dress, how I should talk, how I should sit. Even how I should laugh. My mother says I should laugh softly—like a girl."

Arjun snorted. "Yeah? My dad says I shouldn't laugh too much at all. Says it makes me look unserious. And men should be serious."

Meera rolled her eyes. "Exactly. There's a rule for everything. I can't be loud. You can't be soft. I have to wear clothes that 'cover properly.' You're not even allowed to care about clothes at all, because apparently, that's 'not what boys do.' Who even decided this?"

Arjun shrugged. "I don't know. But I do know that if I cried in front of my uncle, he'd say I was weak."

Meera nudged him. "But you're not weak."

"And you're not improper for laughing too loud," he said, grinning.

She rested her chin on her hands. "It's exhausting, though. Like, what happens if one day, I don't feel like being what they want me to be?"

"You get called difficult," Arjun muttered.

Meera sighed again. "You ever think about how much easier life would be if we just… didn't have to prove anything?"

"Every single day," he said.

They sat in silence for a while, both staring at the sky—where there were no rules.

Here are some questions to reflect upon

How much of who you are today is shaped by the expectations of others, and who might you become if those expectations no longer defined you?

What aspects of your identity have you had to shrink or hide to fit within socially accepted norms?

In what ways do colonial ideas of gender and beauty still influence your everyday choices, consciously or unconsciously?

How can we begin to unlearn the gender roles imposed on us and reclaim a more authentic sense of self?

What would true gender freedom look like—not just for individuals, but for entire communities?

Chapter 4

Medicine and Memory: Healing Through Time

சாகிறவரையில் மருந்து கொடுக்கவேண்டும்
Medicine should be given until death

Whispers of the Healers

They came with their books, their sterile white halls,
Called our healers witches, our wisdom mere calls.
The hands that once traced stars on fevered skin,
Were severed, silenced—erased from within.
They told us our roots were tangled with lies,
That the pulse of the earth could not make us rise.
The herbs, the chants, the fire, the stone,
Replaced by cold steel, and we grieved alone.
Yet beneath the hum of fluorescent light,
The old songs still echo, fierce in their fight.
For medicine is not just what's seen in a chart,
It's the warmth of a hand, the beat of a heart.
So let the past and the present entwine,
Let science and spirit both have their time.
For healing was never meant to divide—
It lives where the old and the new coincide.

For much of human history, healing was a holistic practice, deeply intertwined with culture, spirituality, and the rhythms of nature. Colonial medicine, with its rigid classification of diseases and reliance on pharmaceuticals, systematically dismissed indigenous healing traditions as primitive or unscientific. *Ayurvedic*, *Siddha*, and *Unani* systems—once widely respected—were relegated to the margins, while Western biomedicine became the dominant paradigm.

The medicalization of human experiences meant that grief, spiritual crises, and community-driven healing were reframed as pathologies requiring intervention. This shift severed people from their ancestral knowledge, stripping healing of its relational and spiritual dimensions.

How Trauma, Chronic Illness, and Mental Health Are Understood Across Cultures

Trauma, particularly intergenerational trauma, is often viewed through a Western psychological lens, diagnosed as PTSD or complex PTSD and treated with individual therapy. However, in many indigenous and collectivist cultures, trauma is not merely an individual affliction but a rupture in the communal fabric. Research shows that indigenous groups worldwide—from Native American communities to Dalit populations in India—perceive healing as a communal process involving rituals, storytelling, and collective mourning rather than solitary introspection (Gone, 2013). The erasure of these approaches has led to a mismatch in treatment, where indigenous people seeking mental health support often find Western methods inadequate or alienating (Kirmayer et al., 2011).

Similarly, chronic illness is often understood differently across cultures. In Western medicine, chronic pain or autoimmune diseases are treated primarily through medication and symptom management. In contrast, traditional healing practices, such as *Ayurveda* and Chinese medicine, view chronic conditions as imbalances within the body's energy systems, requiring dietary, lifestyle, and spiritual interventions. Studies indicate that integrating these perspectives can improve patient outcomes—*Ayurvedic* treatments for rheumatoid arthritis, for example, have been found to provide long-term relief in ways conventional medicine alone cannot (Rastogi, 2010).

A Personal Reckoning with Ayurvedic Medicine

I never grew up with *Ayurvedic* medicine. My mother, with her MPhil in Economics, and my father, with his PhD in Physics, built a household where "English medicine" was the usual form of treatment we recognized. For the longest time, I struggled with relentless allergies, waking up every morning to uncontrollable sneezing fits. Modern antihistamines helped, but they never solved the problem. In fact, regular consumption started impacting my gut health.

It was only when my mother-in-law introduced me to *Ayurvedic* remedies that I hesitantly gave them a chance. Skeptical but desperate, I tried them—and to my surprise, they worked. At the age of 27, I would wake up without my nose clogged for two hours. The difference was undeniable, and for that, I will always be grateful. This experience made me question what other traditional remedies I had dismissed—not because they were ineffective, but because I was conditioned to believe they were lesser.

The Gendered Experience of Medicine

Our mothers and grandmothers Women's relationship with medicine has been fraught with exclusion and skepticism. For centuries, medical research excluded women from clinical trials, leading to a significant gap in understanding female physiology and health conditions (Criado-Perez, 2019). Many women hesitate to visit doctors, often dismissing their own pain due to ingrained social conditioning or negative past experiences with medical professionals who downplay their symptoms. This is particularly evident in reproductive health—conditions like endometriosis are still widely underdiagnosed because medical literature has historically centered on male bodies. Meanwhile, childbirth, once a deeply communal and sacred process attended by midwives and healers, became increasingly medicalized, shifting from homes to hospitals. It is undeniable that modern obstetrics has improved maternal mortality, however, it has also alienated women from traditional birthing wisdom, treating pregnancy as a condition to be managed rather than a natural process.

Personally, I have struggled with chronic autoimmune conditions and endometriosis, and much of my healing has come from Western medicine. The advancements in immunology, pain management, and diagnostics have played a crucial role in my ability to function day-to-day. Living with an autoimmune condition means navigating a world where my body often turns against itself—where inflammation, pain, and fatigue are constant companions.

My interactions with doctors, hospitals, and the medical system have shaped my understanding of both the strengths and limitations of modern medicine. It has been an integral part of my life, and while it has offered life-saving treatments, it has also reminded me of the gaps— of how much medicine still does not fully understand, particularly when it comes to conditions that disproportionately affect women and marginalized communities.

Bridging the Gap: Honoring Both Science and Ancestral Healing

The advancements in immunology, pain management, and diagnostics have played a crucial role in my ability to function day-to-day. I have relied on medications that regulate my immune system, physiotherapy that has helped me regain strength, and scientific interventions that have allowed me to live a fuller life. My experience has taught me that healing is not a binary of ancient vs. modern—it is about finding what works. The problem is not that Western medicine exists, but that it has often positioned itself as the *only* valid form of care, dismissing the wisdom of systems that have helped people heal for centuries.

The future of medicine does not have to be a choice between modern science and indigenous wisdom—it can be both. There is space for antibiotics and herbal medicine, for psychotherapy and ritual healing, for hospitals and community-driven care. Decolonizing medicine does not mean rejecting advancements; it means making space for healing traditions that were dismissed, reclaiming the right to engage with both worlds. In a time where integrative medicine is gaining recognition, it is crucial to acknowledge that our ancestors were not ignorant—they understood healing in ways that were relational, cyclical, and deeply intuitive.

Disclaimer: Having worked extensively in the health sector, including within the World Health Organization, I understand the transformative impact of modern medicine. This is not an argument against it. Instead, I am highlighting the loss of the *art* of healing—the aspects of care that were dismissed, the traditions that were deemed inferior, and the healing methods that were erased due to colonial influence. Faith-based healing and indigenous healing practices are valid ways of approaching disease and illness, and recognizing their value does not undermine scientific progress—it enriches it.

Perumaiammal (my late great grandmother) & Sara (my cousin, name changed): A Conversation Across Time that never was

Scene: A quiet afternoon in the ancestral home, the scent of jasmine lingering in the air. Scene: A warm evening in the ancestral home. The air smells of freshly brewed rasam. Perumaiammal sits on the veranda, carefully mixing herbs in a brass bowl. Sara watches, sipping warm ginger tea, a strip of a pain-relief patch stuck to her forehead.

Sara: *("groaning") Perumai, my head is killing me. I've taken two painkillers, but it's still not going away.*

Perumaiammal: *("raising an eyebrow") Poor thing. Your head is fighting something, but you've only told it to be quiet.*

Sara: *("laughing") That's not how medicine works, Perumai! It blocks the pain signals in my brain.*

Perumaiammal: *("thoughtful") Hmm. Blocking pain and healing are not always the same thing, are they?*

Sara: *("sighing") Okay, okay. What would you have done?*

Perumaiammal: *("crushing tulsi leaves in her palm") A little thulasi, some dry ginger, a pinch of omam. Boil it well, drink it warm, and rest. Your body knows how to heal itself, ma. You only have to listen to it.*

Sara: *("frowning") But isn't it better to just take medicine and move on? I have work, classes—there's no time to rest like before.*

Perumaiammal: *("smiling") Ah, that is the real problem, isn't it? Not medicine, but time.*

Sara: *("muttering") Amma says the same thing. But she also only believes in 'English medicine.' She never gave me all this herbal stuff when I was growing up.*

Perumaiammal: *("nodding") Because times changed. And your mother is right too—Western medicine is powerful. It saves lives in ways our herbs never could. But not everything needs a pill. Not every ache must be silenced.*

Sara: *("thoughtful") So... both are important?*

Perumaiammal: *("smiling") Of course, ma. If I had a broken leg, I wouldn't ask you to make me kashayam—I'd want a doctor! But for the small things, the everyday things, our ancestors had wisdom too. Science and tradition are not enemies.*

Sara: *("softly") So maybe instead of choosing between them, we should learn when to use both?*

Perumaiammal: *("nodding") That is all I wanted to hear. Now, come help me grind this omam. If nothing else, it will keep your hands busy while your headache fades.*

Sara rolls her eyes but smiles, knowing that in this moment, across time and tradition, she is learning more than just a remedy.

Sara groans, but they both laugh—two women from different worlds, connected by blood, unbound by time.

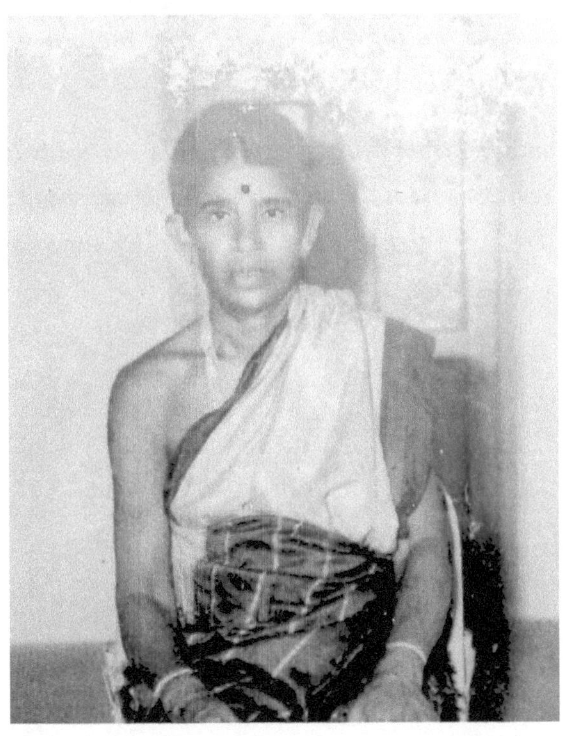

My great grandmother, Perumaiammal

Sara is 11 and if my great grandmother Perumaiammal was alive, she would be a little over 100 years old now.

Here are some reflective questions for the end of this chapter

What does healing mean to you? Is it just the absence of illness, or does it also include emotional, spiritual, and communal well-being?

Have you ever dismissed a traditional remedy or healing practice because it wasn't "scientific"? Where do you think that instinct comes from?

In what ways has colonialism shaped the way you understand medicine and health? Have you ever felt pressured to choose between modern medicine and traditional healing?

How does time affect healing? Do you feel that modern life forces you to "recover" quickly rather than fully heal?

What healing practices from your ancestors would you want to reclaim? And how can they coexist with the advancements of modern medicine?

Chapter 5

Therapy, Healing, and the Wisdom of the Body: Wounds That Speak

வைத்தியன் பாராத நோய் தீருமா?
Can a disease be cured without treatment?

The Reluctance to Heal

They tell me therapy is a foreign thing,
A stranger's voice in a motherland's home.
They say, "We have temples, we have mantras,
Why do we need their sterile rooms and sterile words?"

Once, we sat under banyan trees,
Our pain unraveling like loose threads,
Held in the hands of sages, grandmothers,
Stories woven into healing spells.

Now, they tell me to look Westward,
To couch-bound confessions and textbooks thick with foreign names.
They say, "You must unlearn your ways,
Only science can save you."

But what is science, if not the knowing of one's own wounds?
What is healing, if not the language of our own ancestors?
Perhaps therapy is not the enemy,
But the way it was taken, stripped, and sold back to us—
The Gift in a White Box,

They took our breath and called it *Pranayama,*
Wrapped it in science, gave it back in a white box.
They traced our *kolams*, called them *mandalas*,
Marketed them as mindfulness.

They watched us dance our grief away,
Branded it movement therapy.
They made us forget what was ours,
Then sold it back as enlightenment.
And we?

We learned to doubt our own wisdom,
We learned to fear our own ways—
That is the wound we must reclaim.

The Colonial Origins of Therapy and Mental Health Diagnoses

The field of psychology, as we know it today, was shaped by Western thinkers, most of whom ignored or dismissed non-Western philosophies of mind, emotion, and healing. Colonial rule not only imposed political dominance but also epistemic dominance—it dictated what knowledge was "valid" and what was "superstition." This mindset extended to mental health, where indigenous ways of healing were often pathologized or erased.

For centuries, Tamil healing traditions have recognized the deep connection between mind, body, and environment. **Siddha medicine,** one of the oldest systems of healing in India, emphasized balance through herbal remedies, diet, yoga, and meditation—not just for physical ailments but also for mental well-being.

Tamil folk traditions similarly nurtured emotional resilience through **rituals, storytelling, and communal care.** Sangam literature, particularly texts like *Akananuru* and *Purananuru,* contains vivid depictions of emotional distress—grief, longing, and existential despair—alongside descriptions of how communities supported individuals through poetry, music, and shared wisdom.

However, with the advent of British colonial rule, these indigenous approaches to mental health were **systematically marginalized.** In the 19th century, the British established asylums in India, modeled after Western psychiatric institutions, which often **pathologized traditional healing practices.** Indigenous methods—such as trance healing, ritualistic drumming, and herbal psychiatry—were dismissed as "superstitious" or even criminalized. This shift imposed a **Eurocentric framework of mental health,** divorcing wellness from its historical and cultural context.

Anti-colonial psychiatrist **Frantz Fanon** argued that colonial psychiatry was not merely a medical tool but an instrument of control, shaping how colonized people saw themselves. In India, this influence persisted long after independence, creating a mental health system that often prioritizes Western diagnostic labels over **culturally embedded approaches to healing.** Even today, reclaiming traditional Tamil healing wisdom— alongside modern therapy—offers a powerful path to decolonizing mental health care.

Many dominant therapy models emerged in individualistic societies and were designed with those cultural assumptions in mind—where self-reliance is valued, where healing is an internal process, and where the therapist's office is a private, closed space. Therapy, as we know it today, often assumes that healing *only* happens in solitude, through personal reflection, with a focus on the self.

But India is not an individualistic society. *We have **never** healed in isolation.* Our mental health was woven into the fabric of daily life—in shared experiences, in community care, in rituals passed down through generations.

And yet, when therapy arrived here, it did not adapt to us. Instead, it asked us to adapt to it.

The Diagnostic and Statistical Manual of Mental Disorders (DSM), the global standard for mental health diagnoses, remains deeply rooted in a Eurocentric framework, often failing to account for cultural variations in distress, coping, and recovery..

How Therapy Fails Marginalized and Non-Western Communities

The Cost of Ignoring Collectivist Healing

In a collectivist culture like India, healing has always been communal. But modern therapy asks people to sit in a room and unpack their trauma alone, rather than process it with their family, their community, their people.

We spoke to our kin while cutting vegetables—theraputic.

We gathered under a banyan tree to discuss our struggles—theraputic.

We sat at tea shops, debated, and argued—theraputic.

We tied malli poo in each other's hair while sharing our days—theraputic.

We worked in the fields, hands deep in the soil, breathing in the land of our ancestors—theraputic.

This is what healing looked like for us. But today, we are told that true healing happens in a therapist's office, in a quiet, structured, Western framework that doesn't always make sense to us.

Western therapy models operate on certain assumptions that do not always translate across cultures:

The One-Size-Fits-All Approach: Therapy is often designed with Western patients in mind, assuming universal applicability.

The Language Barrier: Many Indian languages do not have direct translations for Western mental health concepts. The very framing of "mental illness" in a medicalized sense can feel foreign.

Stigma and Mistrust: Therapy is often perceived as something for "the privileged" or "the broken," making it inaccessible to those who might benefit from it most.

Talk Therapy vs. Embodied Healing: Western models prioritize verbal processing, while many Indian traditions emphasize movement, ritual, and spirituality.

My mother and her friends getting ready for a festival

The Rapid Evolution We Were Never Meant For

We were never meant to live like this. We were never meant to sit in front of a screen for 9-5 jobs, consuming and creating endless content. Human beings are not designed for this pace of change. The climate is shifting faster than we can adapt. The air is polluted, the cities are loud, and the pressure to always be productive is crushing.

And yet, when people say, *"Back in my days, we never had all these mental health problems,"*—they fail to see that we are not living in the same world anymore. The weight of modernity, capitalism, and social media is unlike anything previous generations faced. And our mental health is paying the price.

The Illusion of Normality

I see it in my clients every day. Maya, the woman I spoke about in my TEDx talk, walks into my office exhausted, juggling multiple roles—

mother, daughter, wife, employee—trying to be perfect in all of them. Trying to make it look effortless, aesthetic, Instagrammable.

She is not alone. There are so many like her, believing they must carry everything with grace, believing that falling apart is a personal failure rather than a sign of a broken system. They come to therapy looking for solutions, but what they really need is permission to question the system itself.

Reclaiming Therapy for Us

Healing in India cannot be modeled after the West. It cannot be about the individual alone. Therapy, when done in a collectivist way, has the potential to be powerful, to be widely accepted, to feel natural rather than foreign.

We need therapy that integrates our wisdom:

Therapy that happens in circles, in shared spaces, in dialogue, rather than in sterile offices.

Therapy that includes families, that heals relationships, not just individuals.

Therapy that reclaims our traditional ways of movement, music, ritual, and nature as valid forms of healing.

Therapy that understands the weight of rapid change and helps people navigate it, not just cope with it.

We don't need to abandon therapy. But we need to reclaim it, reshape it, and make it ours again. Because healing has always belonged to us—it was never meant to be sold back to us in a white box.

At House of Hibiscus, healing doesn't just happen in therapy rooms— it happens in the way we come together. We host game nights where competitiveness fades into laughter, sing loudly and off-key in rooms filled with voices that drown out self-doubt, and dance with abandon, not for performance but for the sheer joy of movement. We reclaim the spaces that modern life has made rigid—turning them into places of community, spontaneity, and shared experience. Healing is in the togetherness, in the rhythm of collective joy, in the reminders that we were never meant to do this alone.

As a mental health professional, I have a wealth of knowledge to share about therapy, mental health models, and how they can be reshaped to better fit our cultural contexts. But this book is not just about therapy—it is about decolonizing the way we think, the way we see ourselves, and the way we engage with the world. While there is much to be said about reclaiming therapeutic practices, that is a conversation for another book. Here, we will touch upon it briefly, not as an exhaustive guide, but as an invitation to question, to unlearn, and to begin reimagining healing in ways that feel true to us.

A Conversation on Decolonizing Therapy

Setting: *A quiet therapy office. I sit across from my supervisor, discussing a client's struggles with balancing Tamil cultural values and colonial expectations of success and independence.*

Aksheyaa: Supervisor, I wanted to discuss something that's been coming up with one of my clients. She's in her late 20s, unmarried, living with her family, and feeling torn between what she wants and what she's expected to do.

Supervisor: That's quite common. What specifically is she struggling with?

Aksheyaa: It's the whole concept of *thaai veedu*—the maternal home being the center of emotional life. She loves her family, she finds comfort in the rituals of home, in sitting with her mother while she cuts vegetables, in the familiarity of Tamil traditions. But then, there's this nagging guilt that she isn't 'independent enough.' She feels like she should move out, live alone, and be self-sufficient, because that's what 'success' looks like in a Western-influenced world.

Supervisor: Ah. The colonial hangover of individualism.

Aksheyaa: Exactly. She's internalized this idea that to be *truly* successful, she needs to unlearn reliance on her family. But at the same time, she feels deeply unhappy at the thought of leaving behind the closeness, the collective care. She's caught between two worlds—one that values autonomy above all else and another that sees interdependence as a strength.

Supervisor: And why does she feel that independence means distance?

Aksheyaa: Because of the way independence is defined now. The Western model tells her that being successful means separating, that emotional closeness to family is a sign of immaturity. But in our culture, family is an extension of self. Success doesn't have to mean isolation.

Supervisor: Have you spoken to her about how independence can look different?

Aksheyaa: I have. I asked her if she sees her mother as weak because she prioritizes family, and she immediately said no—she admires her strength. That's when she started realizing that she doesn't have to reject Tamil ways of being to be successful.

Supervisor: Good. It's important for her to see that the colonial definition of success is not the only one. In our culture, *being rooted* is a form of strength. The idea that you have to struggle alone to be powerful? That's a very colonial idea.

Aksheyaa: Yes, and it's everywhere—therapy included. So much of what we are taught in our training emphasizes self-sufficiency. I find myself constantly reworking models to fit the realities of my clients.

Supervisor: That's part of decolonizing therapy. You're helping her redefine success, not as an escape from her roots, but as growth within them.

Aksheyaa: Exactly. She doesn't have to choose between being a 'modern, independent woman' and being someone who finds joy in making filter coffee for her father in the morning. Those things aren't opposites.

Supervisor: No, they're not. She's Tamil, and Tamilness is not something to erase for the sake of modernity.

Aksheyaa: Yes. And maybe therapy itself needs to make more space for this—to let people exist in both worlds without feeling like they're failing in either.

Supervisor: That's the work, Aksheyaa. That's the work.

Here are some reflective questions to include at the end of the chapter

How has colonialism shaped your understanding of success, independence, and self-reliance?

In what ways have you felt pressured to conform to Western ideals of mental health and healing?

What aspects of your cultural identity bring you comfort, but have been framed as 'holding you back'?

How do you define strength? Is it through individual achievement, collective care, or both?

Have you ever felt like you had to 'unlearn' parts of your culture to be taken seriously in professional or personal spaces?

What would reclaiming your own definition of healing and well-being look like for you?

Chapter 6

Relearning Love: Beyond Ownership, Beyond Borders

சத்துருக்களையும் சித்தமாய் நேசி.
Love even your enemies heartily.

Love, Before and After

Once, love was a river—
flowing through families, villages, hands that held not just one,
but many.
A grandmother's wisdom, a neighbor's care,
love was never meant to fit inside a home with locked doors.

Then came borders—
not just on land, but in hearts, in homes, in skin.
Love was rewritten in foreign tongues,
measured in diamonds, signed on paper,
folded into the shape of a nuclear family,
until we forgot how to hold each other without ownership.

They told us love was fair skin, thin waists, soft silence.
That a man must provide, a woman must serve.
That a name on a document mattered more

than a name whispered in the wind.
But love was never theirs to define.

Love was once a circle, not a chain.
It was hands calloused from work, but open to care.
It was kin, it was community, it was the strength of many.
Not a contract, not a cage.

So we unlearn.
We love in ways they tried to erase—
with interwoven fingers, with voices unshackled,
with a love too vast to be owned,
too free to be conquered.

The Colonial Inheritance of Beauty, Love, and Marriage

Once, beauty was not a singular standard—it was a spectrum, rich with diversity, deeply rooted in culture, environment, and spiritual significance. In pre-colonial societies, gods were adorned in hues of deep brown and blue-black, reflecting the richness of the land and the people. But colonialism imposed a new gaze—one that deemed fairer skin, straight hair, and thin bodies as the ideal, a mark of proximity to power. This erasure of indigenous beauty standards was deliberate, reinforced through media, education, and commerce. Skin-lightening products, introduced as tools of 'civilization,' continue to fuel billion-dollar industries, their very existence a testament to colonial residue.

Research from Mohanty (1988) in *Under Western Eyes: Feminist Scholarship and Colonial Discourses* highlights how colonial rule imposed Western gender norms, reinforcing the subjugation of women in relationships. The same colonial forces that redefined beauty also reshaped marriage. Where unions were once embedded in communal ties, ensuring familial and societal harmony, they became transactions dictated by European legal frameworks.

Similarly, Loomba (1998) in *Colonialism/Post colonialism* discusses how colonial legal systems institutionalized heteronormative, patriarchal structures, making them appear as natural progressions rather than imposed disruptions. The fluidity of relationships—where marriages were about alliances, kinship, and mutual survival—was replaced by rigid structures where love was secondary to economic and social standing. Arranged marriages, once deeply collaborative and flexible, took on the exploitative tones of dowry exchanges and patriarchal control. Western romantic ideals, fueled by literature and film, introduced a narrative where love meant ownership, where desire meant conquest.

The Western Idea of Love vs. Communal and Interdependent Relationships

Every time we'd visit our native, our neighbour, *Chinnaponnu paati,* my grandmother's best friend, would come home with several home grown gifts and lots of love. However, very often, we don't know our neighbours in our own apartments in urban settings. The nuclear family, a colonial construct, fractured traditional systems of caregiving and support. Where love was once communal—shared between extended families, neighbors, and kin.

However, it became an insular, exclusive dynamic between two individuals. This shift did not happen in isolation; it was fueled by capitalist demands that made economic survival dependent on small, self-sustaining family units rather than interconnected communities.

In indigenous cultures across the world, relationships were not bound by the Western ideals of monogamy and possession. Love was fluid, interwoven with community care. In *Decolonizing Love: Queer Kinship and Settler Colonialism,* Driskill (2010) argues that colonialism not only enforced heteronormativity but also erased queer and non-binary relationship models that were once integral to many cultures. The imposition of legal structures that criminalized same-sex relationships further erased indigenous ways of loving and living.

Marriage, once a means of strengthening communities, was transformed into an economic contract. Studies, such as those by Lugones (2007) in *Heterosexualism and the Colonial/Modern Gender System*, show how colonial powers enforced patriarchal dependency, making men providers and women caregivers, stripping relationships of their earlier shared responsibilities and mutual dependence.

Healing Relationships Through Cultural Reconnection

To decolonize love is to unlearn control, to dismantle possessiveness, and to return to a model of shared care. The Western notion of soulmates—a singular person fulfilling all needs—is an artificial constraint, erasing the broader, interconnected ways of loving that once existed. Indigenous practices of partnership emphasized collective well-being, where responsibilities and emotional support were distributed across extended kin networks rather than being placed solely on one partner.

Reclaiming these traditions does not mean rejecting all modern relationships but rather re-examining the dynamics of love, care, and partnership. Unlearning colonial narratives about marriage, gender roles, and beauty allows us to rebuild relationships rooted in interdependence and authenticity.

As we reconnect with these histories, we begin to heal—not just ourselves, but the generations before us who were forced to forget. Love, once taken from us and reshaped through colonial frameworks, can be ours again, in forms truer to who we are and where we come from.

Decolonizing love is not about rejecting all aspects of modern relationships but about questioning their origins, challenging imposed ideals, and reintroducing cultural ways of love, care, and connection that were erased through colonialism. It is an act of resistance and restoration—one that allows us to move beyond rigid expectations of beauty, marriage, and gender roles and instead build relationships that reflect who we truly are.

By embracing communal care, redefining partnership beyond possession, and acknowledging the fluidity of love, we honor our past while shaping a future that is authentically ours.

Beyond the Binary

South Asian societies held space for a far more fluid and expansive understanding of identity. Indigenous love frameworks were not bound by rigid definitions of man and woman; instead, they acknowledged the existence of non-binary, gender-fluid, and third-gender individuals— many of whom played vital social, spiritual, and cultural roles. Hijras, kinnars, and other gender-diverse communities were historically respected as custodians of sacred knowledge, mediators of blessings, and integral members of familial and social structures.

Love and kinship, too, were shaped by this expansiveness—relationships were not always confined to the heteronormative marriage model but included bonds built on care, chosen kinship, and fluid partnership structures. Colonization imposed Eurocentric norms that erased or criminalized these identities, replacing them with rigid gender and relationship hierarchies. To truly decolonize our understanding of love, we must reclaim these erased histories and recognize that love, in its indigenous form, was always meant to be fluid, inclusive, and affirming of all identities.

What if love was –

Granddaughter: Paati, do you think love was different when you were younger?

Grandmother: *Chuckles*

Grandmother: Love has always been the same, ma. It is people who have changed. Or rather, people have been told to love in different ways.

Granddaughter: What do you mean?

Grandmother: When I was young, love was not just between two people. It was between families, between neighbors. We didn't think of love as something you only give to a husband or a wife. We showed it by sharing food, by raising each other's children, by mourning together, by celebrating together. Now, they say love is between two people only, locked in a house, closed off from the world.

Granddaughter: But isn't that romantic? To have one person who is your everything?

Grandmother: *Shakes head* That is what they want you to believe. That you should put all your hopes, all your dreams, all your burdens on one person. It is a lonely way to love. Before, we spread love so that it never felt like a weight. Now, they tell you that love must be only between two people, and if it fails, you have nothing left.

Granddaughter: You mean the whole 'soulmate' thing?

Grandmother: *Laughs*

Grandmother: Soulmates! Who decided that? The British? The movies? Love was never about finding one person to complete you, ma. You are already whole. Love was about making life easier, about sharing happiness and sorrow. Now they have made it about ownership. That is not love. That is control.

Granddaughter: But isn't it good that we get to choose who we love now? Before, people didn't even have a choice.

Grandmother: That is true, kanmani. We should always choose love. But do you know what else colonialism did? It made marriage a transaction. Before, when two people got married, they didn't just marry each other. They became part of a bigger system, a safety net. Now, they tell you marriage is about just two people—and that is why so many struggle. They made marriage about status, about wealth, about fair skin and good jobs. They made love into something you must earn, instead of something you simply are.

*Granddaughter: *Thinks for a moment* That's true. Even now, so many people look at a person's skin color or salary before saying yes to a marriage.*

Grandmother: Because they were taught to. Before the British came, our gods were dark-skinned, our women were strong, our men were not afraid to cry. Now, they tell you a bride must be fair, a husband must be rich, and that love must look a certain way. They even made us forget how we used to love freely.

*Granddaughter: *Softly* So how do we fix it?*

*Grandmother: *Smiles**

Grandmother: By remembering. By unlearning. By loving the way we were meant to—without shame, without control, without fear. Love is not something to own, ma. It is something to share. And when we share, we are never alone.

Some questions to reflect upon

How has colonialism shaped the way we understand love, relationships, and beauty today?

What aspects of love and marriage in your culture have been altered by Western ideals, and what might they have looked like before?

How does the idea of ownership in relationships impact the way we experience love and partnership?

What would love and marriage look like if they were rooted in community care rather than individualism?

How can we begin to unlearn colonial narratives about love and embrace more interconnected, decolonized ways of loving?

Chapter 7

Before Parenting Was a Battle,
it Was a Village

"செயல் வார்த்தைக்கு மிகுந்தது"
"Actions speak louder than words"

Between Books and Blood

They say, *never raise your voice,*
that a child should grow in whispers,
soft words shaping soft hearts.
But your mother tells you,
"We were raised with firm hands, and we turned out fine."

They say, *gentle hands, gentle words,*
but your father reminds you of the cane,
the weight of discipline, the fear of disobedience—
"Respect is learned through rules, not kindness."

You read about boundaries, autonomy, choice,
but your grandmother scoffs,
"We raised you in a house full of people,
Why do you need so much space?"

Between pages and prayers,
between research and rituals,
between what you were taught and what you now teach—
there is confusion.

You want to raise a child who is free,
but not lost.
Rooted, but not buried.
Strong, but not hardened.

So you listen to the books,
but also to the stories in your mother's voice.
You hold onto wisdom,
but leave behind the wounds.
You teach love,
but without the fear.

And in that space—
between books and blood—
you find your way.

It takes a village to raise a child wasn't just a saying for me—it was my reality. I was raised in Moyalnoor, a place where motherhood was never solitary. The whole village played a role in my upbringing—neighbors who soothed my cries when my mother needed rest, elders who passed down stories and wisdom, and a community that instinctively knew how to share the weight of caregiving.

But today, that village is disappearing. What was once a collective effort has now become an isolated struggle. The burden that was once spread across many shoulders now rests on just two or three, if a mother is lucky. Support networks have shrunk, and what was once a given—

having people to care for both mother and child—is now a privilege. In a world that glorifies independence, we have forgotten that raising a child was never meant to be a one-person job.

Parenting and Colonization: The Struggle Between Past and Present

Parenting has never been simple, but for those navigating the tensions between tradition and modernity, it is an act of constant negotiation. We want to raise our children with love, resilience, and strength—but how do we do so when the very structures of parenting have been shaped by colonial forces? How do we balance the wisdom of our ancestors with the knowledge of contemporary child development? How do we unlearn what was imposed on us while preserving what is worth keeping? These are the questions that define parenting in the wake of colonization.

I sat across from my therapist, my hands curled into my lap, as I voiced a fear I hadn't said out loud before. "I'm scared of becoming a parent," I admitted. "What if it changes everything? What if I lose everything I've built from scratch?"

A fear not unknown to many women.

She listened, then leaned forward, her voice steady and warm. "Women worked in farms not too long ago," she said. "They had children, and as soon as they were well enough, they took their babies to the fields. The entire community took care of the child. When they said it takes a village to raise a child, they didn't mean a handful of people—they meant a whole village. That's the kind of roots we come from." Her words settled in my chest, heavy yet comforting. I had been carrying the weight of parenthood as an individual burden, forgetting that, once, it was never meant to be shouldered alone.

Colonialism disrupted the communal family structures that had long existed in many societies, including Tamil culture, where extended families played a central role in raising children. Traditionally, Tamil households often functioned as joint families, with grandparents, aunts, uncles, and cousins all contributing to childcare and decision-making. This structure provided social support, financial stability, and a sense of belonging.

However, colonial policies—such as the introduction of private property laws, wage labor, and migration for work—fractured these kinship networks. British land reforms in India, for instance, emphasized individual land ownership over collective stewardship, pushing families into nuclear units.

As economic survival became tied to mobility, many moved to cities for work, leaving behind traditional support systems. Today, while nuclear families are the norm, remnants of communal child-rearing persist, such as the reliance on extended family for caregiving and decision-making, reflecting an ongoing negotiation between colonial legacies and indigenous practices.

The Colonial Influence on Parenting Norms

Before colonization, parenting was not a singular or isolated responsibility—it was a communal effort. Extended families, kin networks, and even entire villages shared in the care, discipline, and guidance of children. Parenting was not about control but about teaching through storytelling, observation, and hands-on experience. Children were seen as active participants in their communities, learning through interaction rather than through rigid structures.

Colonial rule disrupted this balance. European influence introduced an authoritarian model of parenting, where discipline, obedience, and hierarchy became the cornerstones of child-rearing. Research by Fanon (1961) in *The Wretched of the Earth* highlights how colonial education systems instilled obedience and conformity, discouraging indigenous child-rearing practices that emphasized communal learning and autonomy.

Similarly, Nyamnjoh (2012) in *Blinded by Sight: Divining the Future of Anthropology* discusses how colonial regimes enforced family structures that diminished the role of community in raising children. The nuclear family—parents and children living in isolation—replaced the communal upbringing that had long existed. The idea that children must be shaped through strict discipline, often enforced through corporal punishment, was deeply embedded into colonial schooling systems and religious institutions. These practices were absorbed into many cultures, passed down through generations as the "proper" way to raise children.

The Push and Pull Between Tradition and Modernity

Parenting today is often a struggle between past and present, between what we were taught and what we now know. There is guilt in rejecting certain traditional practices, especially when they are tied to our cultural heritage, but there is also an urgent need to protect children from oppressive norms that no longer serve them.

Western parenting philosophies, such as "gentle parenting," emphasize emotional intelligence, autonomy, and negotiation rather than control. However, these approaches are often framed as new despite having roots in many indigenous and non-Western cultures, where guidance and emotional nurturing have long been central to child-rearing. Additionally, gentle parenting assumes access to privilege—financial stability, time, and societal support—that may not be available to many parents in post-colonial societies. Raising children in these contexts requires a delicate balance: fostering emotional well-being while equipping them for a competitive, capitalist world that often values discipline and conformity over individuality.

There is an additional struggle of perception. Many elders see newer parenting approaches as "soft" or ineffective, viewing strict discipline as necessary for survival. But should we measure success by endurance alone? Is resilience only valid if it is forged through suffering? These are questions many parents wrestle with as they attempt to redefine what it means to raise strong, compassionate children.

Unlearning Colonial Parenting & Reclaiming Indigenous Wisdom

To move forward, we must first question what we have inherited.

Why do we equate strict discipline with love?

Why do we see obedience as a sign of good parenting?

Why do we emphasize respect for elders but rarely teach elders to respect children?

Unlearning colonial parenting does not mean rejecting all traditional wisdom. Instead, it means reclaiming the nurturing, communal, and intuitive practices that were lost or suppressed. Indigenous storytelling, play-based learning, and mentorship from elders all played crucial roles in pre-colonial child-rearing. Many of these practices align with modern psychology, reinforcing that children learn best in environments of trust, patience, and engagement rather than fear.

How Can We Parent Without Perpetuating Colonial Trauma?

Breaking the cycle of colonial trauma in parenting means questioning, unlearning, and rebuilding. It means raising emotionally resilient children without reinforcing harmful gender roles, allowing boys to be soft and girls to be strong. It means encouraging independence without isolating children from their roots. It means teaching children respect, not through fear, but through example.

Some guiding principles for decolonizing parenting include:

Replacing Control with Guidance: Teaching children through example and conversation rather than strict authority. Instead of enforcing blind obedience, parents can model the behavior they want their children to adopt. For example, rather than punishing a child for speaking rudely, a parent can gently say, "Let's try that again with kindness," and show them how to express frustration in a respectful way. In many indigenous traditions, storytelling was used to guide behavior—rather than saying "Don't lie," elders would share stories where honesty led to strength and wisdom, allowing children to internalize lessons through narrative rather than fear.

Emphasizing Community Over Isolation: Allowing extended family and trusted elders to play active roles in child-rearing. In many cultures before colonial rule, children were raised by an entire community, not just their immediate parents. Grandparents, aunts, uncles, and even neighbors played key roles in nurturing and disciplining children. For example, in many African and Indigenous American traditions, a child's well-being was considered the responsibility of the whole village. If a child misbehaved, guidance would come from a trusted elder rather than just the parent, reinforcing collective responsibility and support. This is in stark contrast to the Western nuclear family model, which isolates parents and places immense pressure on them to be everything for their child.

2 men played a very important role in raising me in my early childhood

My great grandfather, Mariappan and my grandfather, Jayaprakasan.

There were a lot more women who raised me but these 2 men did not think it was a women's role to take care of me. They fed me, bathed me, played with me and put me to sleep – not just when the women were busy but even otherwise.

Reclaiming Cultural Practices: Introducing children to indigenous storytelling, languages, and rituals that foster identity and belonging. Many colonized societies were forced to abandon their languages, traditions, and spiritual practices, disconnecting generations from their roots. Parents today can actively reclaim these by teaching their children indigenous lullabies, celebrating traditional festivals, or telling bedtime stories rooted in their own ancestry. For example, in Tamil culture, stories of *Avvaiyar*—an elderly poet and philosopher—teach wisdom through parables, rather than Eurocentric fairy tales that center princesses and knights. Learning one's mother tongue, participating in traditional art forms, or even eating traditional foods can help a child feel a deep sense of identity and belonging.

Raising Emotionally Intelligent Children: Teaching emotional regulation and self-awareness rather than suppression and submission.

Colonial rule often reinforced parenting practices that prioritized obedience over emotional well-being, embedding discipline and hierarchy into child-rearing. Many of us grew up hearing "Stop crying" or "Be strong" rather than being guided through our emotions. While strict parenting existed in some pre-colonial traditions, colonialism intensified and universalized these models, often devaluing indigenous approaches that emphasized emotional development. Shifting away from this means teaching children to name their feelings, validate their experiences, and develop healthy coping strategies. For example, rather than dismissing a child's frustration with "You're overreacting," a parent might say, "I can see that you're really upset. Let's talk about what's making you feel this way." This approach doesn't make children "soft"; it equips them with emotional resilience—helping them navigate challenges without internalizing shame.

Balancing Survival with Emotional Well-being: Preparing children for real-world challenges while ensuring they do not equate struggle with worth. For generations, survival has been prioritized over emotional well-being—children were taught to endure hardship as a sign of strength. While resilience is important, it's equally crucial that children understand they are worthy regardless of how much they suffer. For example, instead of telling a child, "Life is hard, and you just have to deal with it," parents can say, "Yes, life can be challenging, but you deserve joy and rest too." Teaching children to work hard while also valuing rest, creativity, and self-care ensures they don't grow up equating their worth with productivity alone—a deeply ingrained colonial mindset that still lingers today.

Parenting is a dynamic process, and there is no single "right" way to do it. But when we pause to reflect on what we want to pass down, we can choose to keep what strengthens us and let go of what no longer serves us. By honoring the best of our traditions while embracing progress, we can raise children who are not just survivors of history, but creators of a better future.

Parenting in the post-colonial world is not about choosing between the past and the present—it is about weaving them together in a way that nurtures both heritage and growth. We do not need to throw away our traditions, nor do we need to accept everything that was forced upon us. Instead, we can reimagine parenting in a way that allows our children to be free, but never lost; independent, but never alone; rooted, but never confined. In doing so, we offer them the greatest gift: the ability to grow into themselves without the weight of history binding them down.

A little story

In a cozy living room a young father, Rahul, is sitting on the couch, rocking his newborn daughter to sleep. His mother, Lakshmi, watches him with a warm but slightly skeptical expression.

Lakshmi: (smiling)

You're a natural with her, Rahul. But don't you think it's time you hand her over to Priya? She must be tired after feeding her.

Rahul: (gently stroking his daughter's tiny fingers)

Priya is taking a nap, Amma. She barely gets any sleep as it is. And besides, why should only she take care of the baby? She's our daughter, not just her responsibility.

Lakshmi: (sighs)

I know, I know. But this is how it's always been, kanna. Mothers take care of babies, and fathers take care of providing. That's how we raised you too.

Rahul: (soft chuckle)

Exactly. And I barely got to see Appa when I was little. He worked so much that I don't even remember playing with him until I was older. I don't want that for my daughter.

Lakshmi: (softens)

That's true…He was always working. But that's what fathers do.

Rahul: (shaking his head)

Amma, who decided that? Who said fathers can't be nurturing and mothers can't provide? That's just something we've been told for generations. But it's not a rule. It's just a story we keep repeating.

Lakshmi: (thoughtful)

I suppose… But won't people talk? They'll say Priya is making you do all the work. They'll say she isn't a good mother.

Rahul: (firmly)

And that's the problem, Amma. A mother is only "good" if she sacrifices herself? And a father is only "strong" if he stays distant? That's not love—that's just outdated expectations.

Lakshmi: (quietly)

I never thought of it that way… I was exhausted when I had you. But I never complained. It was just my duty.

Rahul: (gently)

You shouldn't have had to do it alone, Amma. You deserved rest, too. And that's why I want things to be different now. My daughter will grow up knowing that her father will always be there for her, not just as a provider, but as a parent.

Lakshmi: (smiling softly)

Thinking back, my grandfather actually used to finish working in the field to come take care of my mother. Back then, he supported her in various ways to ensure she was taken care. Somewhere along the line we've lost that.

Maybe… Maybe it's time we stop worrying about what people will say and just do what's best for our children.

Rahul: *grinning* You've always said I am more like your grandfather than you or appa. I guess, I was reborn as him to pass down this wisdom to you.

They both look down at the baby, who yawns in her sleep, safe and loved in her father's arms.

Here are some questions for you to think about

How has colonialism influenced the way discipline and obedience are perceived in parenting today?

In what ways can parents balance the wisdom of their ancestors with modern psychological insights on child development?

What are some indigenous parenting practices that were lost due to colonization, and how can they be reclaimed?

How can parents shift from a control-based approach to a guidance-based approach while still setting necessary boundaries?

What role does community play in raising emotionally resilient children, and how can parents integrate communal parenting in a modern world?

How can we redefine resilience in parenting so that children grow up strong without equating suffering with worth?

Chapter 8

Till Death Do Us Together

பிறந்த அன்றே இறக்கவேண்டும்.
The day of birth leads to death.

Till Death Do Us Together
They said grief was a private thing,
a silent war behind closed doors,
but my ancestors wailed to the wind,
their sorrow stitched into the soil.

Once, we let the earth hold our tears,
bathed the dead in sandalwood smoke,
sang their names till they became stars,
never gone, only returning home.

But now, they ask us to move on,
to package loss in clean white sheets,
to whisper eulogies without trembling,
to grieve as if we were never whole.

Yet I remember—
Grief is not exile.

It is the thread that ties us to the ones we've loved,
pulling us closer, even in death.

Colonialism and the Suppression of Grief

Grief was never meant to be silent.

Before colonial rule, mourning was a communal act, woven into the rhythms of life. We did not hide our sorrow behind closed doors or shrink it into brief, quiet ceremonies. We wailed, we sang, we told stories of the ones we lost, their names carried in the wind and the waters. Death was not a sudden severance but a passage—one that the living and the dead walked together, bound by ritual, memory, and love.

While **Tamil culture, African traditions, and many indigenous communities embraced expressive grieving,** some societies (including early Buddhist and Confucian traditions) emphasized **quiet, meditative mourning** even before colonialism. **Grief expressions varied across cultures but that colonialism imposed Western norms is "universal."**

As Mohanty (1988) observes in *Under Western Eyes: Feminist Scholarship and Colonial Discourses*, indigenous communities embraced emotional expression as a vital component of healing and cultural continuity. However, with the advent of colonial rule, these rich mourning practices were systematically suppressed in favor of Western stoicism.

Where once our ancestors grieved in the embrace of their communities, colonial rule pushed grief into institutions—the church, the courtroom, the asylum. Loomba (1998) in *Colonialism/Postcolonialism* details how colonial powers redefined natural grief as an aberration—an excessive emotion that required control and regulation

Loss became something to endure in isolation, a quiet suffering rather than a shared passage. Rosenblatt (2008), in *Grief Across*

Cultures, explores how colonial disruptions systematically dismantled indigenous mourning practices, reframing them as irrational or excessive. Similarly, Linda Tuhiwai Smith's work on decolonization highlights how Western frameworks erased indigenous emotional expression, categorizing traditional grief rituals as pathological rather than as vital, culturally embedded processes of remembrance. As a result, colonial institutions imposed rigid, institutionalized forms of mourning—characterized by silent, formal funerals within church walls—that erased the communal, transformative power of grief and severed vital links to ancestral heritage.

Consequently, colonial institutions imposed rigid, institutionalized forms of mourning—characterized by silent, formal funerals within church walls—that erased the communal, transformative power of grief and severed vital links to ancestral heritage. And in doing so, they did not just take our rituals; they took away our way of healing

Death and the Capitalist Machine

Beyond mourning, capitalism has reshaped the very way we care for the dying and elderly. Colonial economic structures laid the groundwork for the fragmentation of family units, which later evolved into modern institutionalized elderly care. Where multi-generational households once provided emotional and social continuity, colonial economic structures fractured family units, forcing elderly care into institutions modeled after European workhouses. The rise of nursing homes and elderly isolation reflects this legacy, prioritizing productivity over kinship (Tronto, 1993).

In contemporary society, grief has become a commodified experience, with the funeral industry transforming loss into a profitable enterprise.. This commercialization extends beyond funerals to encompass insurance policies and the medicalization of bereavement, often framing natural grieving processes as conditions requiring intervention. In many formerly colonized societies, the push for Western modernity meant abandoning collective caregiving in favor of nuclear family setups.

The shift from traditional multi-generational households to institutionalized elderly care facilities exemplifies the dehumanization inherent in capitalist systems. Modern life further exacerbates this by pressuring individuals to "move on" swiftly after a loss, driven by work commitments and a cultural emphasis on productivity over personal well-being. This transition often results in the isolation of the elderly, stripping them of familial bonds and community support.

The question remains: can we reclaim death from the capitalist machine and return it to the hands of the community?

Traditional Mourning Practices

For centuries, Tamil mourning traditions were deeply rooted in community and ritual. Death was not just a private loss but a collective transition, marked by open grieving, ancestor worship, and acts of remembrance. Families would engage in **Oppari** (lament songs) to express their sorrow, a tradition that allowed both the grieving and the larger community to process loss together. Women, in particular, played a significant role in these expressions, yet their grief was often scrutinized—too little mourning was seen as unnatural, while too much was labeled as hysteria.

In Tamil society, pre-colonial literature and poetry allowed for men to grieve openly (e.g., Sangam poetry depicted warriors and kings mourning fallen comrades), but Western influence slowly erased this vulnerability.

Tamil mourning traditions have long been shaped by both indigenous and external influences. Sangam literature (circa 300 BCE–300 CE) offers numerous depictions of men openly expressing grief, from warriors lamenting fallen comrades to kings mourning lost loved ones. Emotional vulnerability was not seen as a weakness but as a testament to deep bonds and honor.

However, even before colonial rule, Brahmanical patriarchy played a role in discouraging overt male emotional expression, particularly among upper-caste groups, where self-restraint and detachment were idealized. British colonial rule further intensified these norms by imposing Victorian ideals of masculinity, which equated emotional suppression with strength and self-discipline.

This colonial reinforcement, combined with existing patriarchal structures, gradually eroded the space for men to grieve openly, particularly in public and ritual contexts. Today, the expectation for men to be stoic in the face of loss persists, though traditional expressions of grief—such as oppari (lament songs) and communal mourning—continue to offer spaces for emotional release. Recognizing this layered history allows for a more nuanced understanding of how Tamil mourning practices have evolved under intersecting cultural and colonial influences.

The pressure to be the "pillar" of the family after a death leads to emotional suppression, often manifesting as anger, detachment, or overwork.

The Spiritual and Cultural Understanding of Death

Tamil literature and folklore have long understood death as a transition rather than an end. **Sangam poetry** speaks of warriors falling in battle not as lives lost, but as spirits joining the eternal flow of existence. Folk traditions depicted the deceased as continuing to walk among the living, guiding and protecting future generations. These narratives provided a sense of continuity, where death was not a rupture but a transformation.

However, colonial religious impositions introduced a more rigid dichotomy—heaven and hell, salvation and damnation—fracturing indigenous beliefs that saw death as a cyclical journey rather than a linear conclusion. Missionary efforts demonized ancestral worship, turning rituals of remembrance into acts of "idolatry." Over time, these shifts distanced people from their own cultural understanding of loss, forcing them to grieve within the confines of colonial frameworks.

Grieving in the Modern World

Today, grief manifests differently in collectivist and individualist cultures. In many Tamil households, mourning remains a shared experience, but the pressures of modernity—migration, urbanization, and nuclear family structures—have made loss an increasingly lonely process. Where once entire villages gathered to support the bereaved, today's grieving person may be expected to process their pain in silence, balancing work obligations with societal expectations to "move on."

The challenge now is to reclaim ancestral ways of mourning while adapting to contemporary realities. Rituals such as *tithi* **(death anniversaries),** *kollam* **(memorial art), and feeding the poor in the name of the departed** remain acts of remembrance that resist colonial erasure. Finding ways to integrate these traditions into modern life allows for a more holistic approach to grief, one that honors the past while acknowledging the present.

Finding Meaning After Loss

Decolonizing grief means rejecting the hurried, sanitized mourning process imposed by colonial and capitalist structures. It means allowing **slowness, ritual, and remembrance** to take precedence over productivity and suppression. **Storytelling remains one of the most powerful ways to keep those we have lost alive.** Through oral histories, songs, and memories passed down, ancestors continue to live within us.

Honoring the dead can also be an act of resistance. By reclaiming ancestral mourning practices—whether through ritual, art, or communal remembrance—we actively challenge the colonial erasure of our cultural expressions of grief. In remembering, we reclaim. In grieving, we reconnect.

Disclaimer: Honoring Without Glorifying

While this chapter discusses the erasure of indigenous mourning practices due to colonial influence, it is important to recognize that not all pre-colonial customs were humane or equitable. Some traditions—such as *sati* (the forced immolation of widows), the seclusion of mourning women, and rigid caste-based funeral restrictions—were deeply harmful and should not be romanticized or revived in the name of cultural reclamation.

Decolonizing grief does not mean a blind return to the past; it means critically reclaiming practices that foster healing, connection, and remembrance while discarding those that reinforced oppression. The goal is not to undo history but to move forward with a nuanced understanding—one that honors our ancestors without repeating their mistakes.

Chinnaponnu paati, our neighbour

I recently lost someone who was like a grandmother to me. Her name was Chinnaponnu. She was a wonderful human being. She was kind, warm and generous. She was my grandmother's best friend and held so much love for my family and I. It was a devastating day for everyone involved.

I entered the funeral in silence, holding myself together with the kind of poise I thought grief demanded. I told myself I was here to pay my respects, to be still, to be strong. But as I stepped inside, the air was thick with loss— not just mine, but everyone's. The weight of a life no longer present, pressed into me.

And then the stories began. People spoke of her—of the laughter she carried, the kindness she poured into the world, the little things she did that now lived only in memory. With every word, my stomach clenched tighter. Why were they telling me all this? Why were they making me remember things that could never happen again? Why did grief feel like someone was slowly wringing my heart dry?

But then, something shifted. The ache didn't lessen, but it changed. The pain wasn't just mine anymore—it was shared. In the telling, in the remembering, she became more than just an absence. She became real again, even if just for a moment. And I understood. Grief isn't just about loss. It's about love, stretched across time, refusing to be forgotten.

Here are some questions for you to ponder about

How have the mourning traditions in your family or culture shaped the way you process grief?

Have you ever felt pressured to grieve in a certain way? How did that affect your healing process?

In what ways has colonial influence changed how we talk about and experience death?

How can we reclaim communal grieving practices while balancing modern responsibilities?

What are some personal or cultural rituals you could create to honor and remember those you've lost?

Chapter 9

Remembering and Rebuilding

Who am I, if not a name in two tongues,
One given, one taken—both heavy on my skin?
A history whispered in borrowed words,
Yet my mother's voice still lingers within.
They told me to rise, but only their way,
To speak, but only in softened sounds.
Success was a road that led me away,
While home was a past that weighed me down.
But what if my roots are not chains, but wings?
What if my tongue is a river, not rust?
What if I am whole, not torn between things—
A name, a land, a life I can trust?
So I walk, not back, not away, but through,
Gathering fragments they told me to lose.
Not unlearning, but remembering anew,
This is my story. This is what I choose.

Rebuilding from Decolonization: The Path to Reclaiming

Decolonization is not just about understanding history—it is about unlearning, reclaiming, and reshaping the way we see ourselves and the world around us. It is a process of peeling back layers of conditioning, questioning what we've been taught to value, and making space for identities that have been erased or suppressed. This is not an easy journey, nor is it a linear one. But it is necessary.

For many of us, colonial narratives live within us so deeply that we don't recognize them as foreign. They shape the way we see beauty, intelligence, and success. They dictate what we aspire to, how we speak, and even how we measure our self-worth. To reclaim ourselves, we must first recognize these narratives—where they come from, how they shape us, and why they persist.

Beyond recognition, there is reconnection. Colonization fractured our relationship with our own knowledge systems—our languages, our traditions, our ways of healing. Many of us grew up distant from the wisdom of our ancestors, believing that progress meant leaving the past behind. But what if the past holds the very tools we need to move forward? What if reclaiming indigenous practices—our languages, our stories, our ways of knowing—is not regression, but a return to wholeness?

A core aspect of this process is redefining success and identity on our own terms. We have inherited ideas that equate success with Western validation—prestigious degrees, high-paying jobs, fluency in English, global mobility. But whose definition of success is this? Who benefits when we abandon our communities, our cultures, our roots? Reclaiming means challenging these imposed values and asking: What do I define as success? What does my community need to thrive?

Unlearning colonial frameworks is not just an intellectual exercise—it is deeply emotional. The wounds of colonization run through generations, manifesting as shame, anxiety, and disconnection. Healing means acknowledging the trauma carried in our families, our communities, and our bodies. It means understanding that our struggles are not personal failures but echoes of a history designed to make us feel small.

And most importantly, decolonization does not always have to be a grand act of resistance. Sometimes, it is in the smallest, most personal choices. It is in the words we choose to use, the stories we pass down, the pride we take in our names, our skin, our heritage. It is in the decision to question, to challenge, to refuse. It is in the act of remembering, every single day.

Reclaiming is not about going back in time—it is about moving forward with awareness, with intention, and with a deep sense of self. This chapter is an invitation to begin.

How Professionals Can Integrate Decolonial Practices

Therapists and Mental Health Professionals

Modern psychology has been deeply shaped by Western diagnostic frameworks, often reducing mental health to individual pathology rather than considering the broader social, cultural, and historical contexts that shape well-being. In many parts of the world, including India, colonial rule disrupted indigenous healing traditions, replacing them with Eurocentric models that prioritize standardized diagnoses over lived experiences. To integrate decolonial practices, therapists must critically examine how these frameworks may overlook the impact of intergenerational trauma, caste-based discrimination, and community-oriented understandings of mental health. Moving beyond Western models means recognizing that distress is not always rooted in cognitive distortions or chemical imbalances but can be deeply linked to historical oppression, cultural alienation, and systemic inequities.

A decolonial approach to therapy requires centering culturally relevant healing practices and acknowledging the limitations of talk therapy alone. Many communities have long relied on storytelling, ritual, spirituality, and collective care as therapeutic tools—practices that modern psychology often dismisses as unscientific. Integrating these into mental health work does not mean rejecting evidence-based approaches but expanding them. Therapists can collaborate with traditional healers, incorporate indigenous wisdom into their practice, and offer therapeutic interventions that respect the cultural realities of their clients. Ultimately, decolonizing therapy is about shifting from a deficit-based model—where clients are seen as "broken" and in need of fixing—to one that honors their resilience, history, and identity.

Doctors and Healthcare Professionals

Decolonizing medicine is about integrating indigenous knowledge with modern medical advancements rather than blindly reviving traditional practices. While many indigenous healing methods offer valuable insights, some, like mercury-based treatments, require critical scrutiny to ensure safety and effectiveness.

The legacy of colonization is deeply embedded in medical systems, influencing everything from diagnostic biases to treatment disparities. Medical racism—where certain populations receive lower-quality care due to racial, caste, or ethnic prejudices—remains a pressing issue in many former colonies, including India.

Medical racism in India is deeply intertwined with casteism, which remains a major structural issue in healthcare (Gupta, 2012). Dalits and Adivasis face systemic neglect, from inadequate access to medical facilities to discrimination by healthcare providers (Deshpande, 2017). Studies reveal that they experience higher mortality rates, are less likely to receive timely medical intervention, and often face humiliation in hospitals. Caste-based biases within medical institutions also influence medical education and patient care, leading to disparities in treatment. Acknowledging caste discrimination as a structural barrier is essential to addressing medical racism in India.

Colonial medicine often treated indigenous bodies as experimental subjects, devaluing traditional healing practices and prioritizing Western biomedical approaches. Today, these biases persist in the form of dismissing patients' pain, pathologizing cultural health practices, and assuming that Western medical knowledge is universally applicable. Addressing these issues requires healthcare professionals to critically examine their training and biases, actively working against discriminatory treatment patterns.

Decolonizing healthcare also means integrating traditional and indigenous healing methods into mainstream medical practice. Many indigenous health systems—such as Ayurveda, Siddha, and Unani medicine—have long emphasized holistic well-being, preventive care, and a deep connection between body, mind, and environment. Rather than treating these as inferior or pseudoscientific, medical professionals can engage with them in a way that respects their legitimacy and historical significance. A shift towards community-driven care, where patients are seen as active participants rather than passive recipients of treatment, is crucial. This means valuing lived experiences, challenging pharmaceutical dependency, and understanding that healing is not just about curing illness but fostering long-term wellness in a culturally rooted way.

Educators and Academics

Education has long been a tool of colonization, used to erase indigenous knowledge and impose Eurocentric worldviews. In India, colonial schooling systems devalued local languages, histories, and intellectual traditions, replacing them with a curriculum that prioritized British literature, Western philosophy, and colonial narratives of progress. Today, many educational institutions continue to uphold these biases, teaching history from a Eurocentric perspective and marginalizing indigenous and local epistemologies. To decolonize education, educators must critically examine the content they teach—who is being centered, whose voices are missing, and how knowledge is being framed. This involves challenging the idea that Western theories are universally applicable and making space for indigenous wisdom, oral histories, and non-Western philosophies.

Decolonizing pedagogy goes beyond curriculum content—it also requires rethinking teaching methods. Many colonial education systems emphasize rote memorization, hierarchy, and rigid assessment models, leaving little room for critical engagement and collaborative learning. A decolonial approach shifts the focus from passive absorption of knowledge to active questioning, discussion, and contextual application. This means valuing students' lived experiences, encouraging multilingual expression, and fostering a learning environment where diverse ways of knowing are respected. Ultimately, decolonizing education is about empowering students to think critically about history, identity, and power—equipping them not just with knowledge, but with the tools to reclaim their own narratives.

Leaders and Organizations

Colonial structures continue to shape modern workplaces, influencing everything from leadership styles to decision-making hierarchies. Many corporate and nonprofit spaces operate under a top-down model, where authority is concentrated in a small, elite group, mirroring colonial governance. This approach often excludes marginalized voices and reinforces power imbalances. Decolonizing leadership requires a fundamental shift towards more inclusive, participatory decision-making processes. Instead of imposing solutions from the top, leaders should prioritize collaboration, recognizing that those closest to a problem often have the best insights on how to solve it. Community-driven leadership models, inspired by indigenous governance systems, emphasize shared responsibility, consensus-building, and horizontal structures rather than rigid hierarchies.

Organizations must also rethink their approach to social impact and development work. Too often, development initiatives replicate colonial patterns, where resources and expertise flow from the "global North" to the "global South" in a charity-based model that frames marginalized communities as helpless recipients rather than active agents of change. A decolonial approach moves away from this paternalistic mindset and towards true empowerment—ensuring that communities have control over their own narratives, resources, and solutions. Ethical storytelling plays a crucial role here; organizations must move away from exploitative representations of suffering and instead amplify voices in a way that is dignified, self-determined, and rooted in justice. Decolonizing leadership is not just about changing policies—it is about fundamentally shifting how power, knowledge, and resources are distributed in ways that challenge colonial legacies.

Future Vision: What Does a Truly Decolonized Mind Look Like?

A decolonized mind is not simply one that has shed colonial narratives—it is one that has actively reimagined and reclaimed ways of being that exist outside imposed binaries. Colonialism fragmented identities, forcing people into rigid categories of race, caste, gender, and class, shaping how we see ourselves and each other. A decolonized mind embraces fluidity and intersectionality, recognizing that identity is not a fixed box but a dynamic, evolving experience shaped by history, culture, and community. It allows us to move beyond narrow definitions of success, beauty, and worth, embracing the multiplicity of ways to exist in the world.

At the heart of decolonization is a return to community-centered living. Colonial systems enforced hyper-individualism, prioritizing competition over cooperation, self-interest over collective well-being. A decolonized society reclaims the balance between individual agency and communal responsibility, recognizing that true liberation is not just personal but collective. It values interdependence, where success is not measured by accumulation but by contribution, where care work is recognized as essential, and where healing happens not in isolation but through shared connection.

Language and storytelling are central to this reclamation. Colonialism erased indigenous tongues, replacing them with languages of power that shaped thought itself. A decolonized world is one where lost languages are revived, where oral traditions are respected as knowledge systems, and where narratives once silenced are reclaimed. It is a world where history is no longer told from the perspective of the colonizer, but through the voices of those who resisted, survived, and thrived.

Economic sovereignty is another pillar of true decolonization. Colonial capitalism extracted wealth from indigenous lands and people, creating systems that continue to widen global inequalities. A decolonized future moves beyond exploitative economies, reimagining systems that prioritize sustainability, fair redistribution, and local autonomy. It embraces economic models rooted in community, where success is measured by well-being rather than profit margins, where indigenous craftsmanship and labor are valued, and where no nation or people are dependent on the economic structures of their former colonizers.

Finally, a decolonized mind is one that is mentally and emotionally free from the weight of colonial legacies. It is a mind that does not seek validation from colonial standards of intelligence, professionalism, or beauty. It is a mind that does not measure its worth by its proximity to whiteness, Western ideals, or capitalist productivity. Instead, it finds worth in its own history, its own culture, and its own people. To decolonize is not just to resist—it is to reimagine, to reclaim, and to build a world where freedom is not given by those in power, but created by those who dare to dream beyond it.

Rebuilding from Decolonization starts at home. It starts with you.

Disclaimer: Decolonization is Not a Return to Oppression

Decolonization is not about romanticizing the past or reviving every aspect of pre-colonial traditions without question. It is not about discarding modern advancements or reverting to oppressive systems that existed before colonial rule. Instead, it is a process of critically reclaiming and reviving the aspects of our cultures that foster equity, respect, and collective well-being while consciously rejecting practices that perpetuate harm, discrimination, or inequality.

Many cultures across the world—including those that were colonized—have historically upheld practices that were deeply patriarchal, exclusionary, or violent. Gender-based oppression, caste hierarchies, and rigid social structures existed before colonial rule, though they were often intensified or reshaped by it. The goal of decolonization is not to uncritically embrace everything that existed before, but to engage in thoughtful reflection about what should be carried forward and what should be left behind.

For instance, draconian gender-related practices such as *Sati* (the forced self-immolation of widows), foot binding, female genital mutilation (FGM), bride kidnapping, and honor killings have caused immense harm and suffering. These were not acts of cultural empowerment; they were instruments of control and subjugation, often justified by patriarchal interpretations of tradition. Similarly, the dowry system, witch hunts, and purity culture reinforced the idea that women's lives, bodies, and choices were not their own. These practices—regardless of their historical or cultural roots—have no place in a decolonized future.

The British colonial administration outlawed *sati* under the guise of moral reform, but their approach was deeply hypocritical. While they condemned the practice as barbaric, they also exoticized it—turning it into a spectacle that reinforced their portrayal of Indian culture as inherently savage and in need of "civilizing." Colonial records, literature, and artwork often sensationalized *sati*, depicting Indian women as passive victims and Indian men as cruel oppressors, conveniently ignoring the complex socio-religious factors at play. This narrative served a dual purpose: it justified British intervention as a supposed moral duty while simultaneously erasing the agency of Indian reformers who were already challenging the practice. In reality, *sati* abolition was not merely a colonial imposition; Indian activists, including Raja Ram Mohan Roy, played a crucial role in advocating against it. Yet, by monopolizing the discourse around *sati*, the British reinforced their self-proclaimed role as benevolent rulers, masking the exploitative realities of their regime.

Decolonization is about discernment. It is about recognizing that culture is not static—it evolves, and we have the power to shape it in ways that honor our histories while upholding human dignity and justice. It means reviving indigenous knowledge systems, community-centered ways of living, and holistic healing practices that were suppressed by colonial rule, while simultaneously discarding traditions that violate bodily autonomy, restrict freedom, or perpetuate violence.

A decolonized world is not one that blindly glorifies the past, nor is it one that unquestioningly follows Western ideals. It is a world where we reclaim what serves us, transform what needs change, and build something that is not just traditional, but truly just.

Final Conversation: A Book, a Legacy, and a Promise

My grandmother, Kalaibagyam, is not just the woman who raised me—she is the foundation of who I am. She is the hands that held me when I cried, the voice that told me stories at night, and the quiet strength that shaped my understanding of love, resilience, and identity.

I call her *Amma*, because she was more than just a grandmother; she was a mother to me in every way that mattered. She taught me how to navigate a world that often felt too sharp, too rigid. And now, as I write this book, I realize that so much of what I am trying to unlearn, she had already questioned long before me. She just never had the privilege of putting it into words the way I do now.

One evening, as I sat by her side, typing away at my manuscript, she watched me with that knowing look—the one that meant she had something to say but was waiting for me to ask. So, I did.

Me: *Smiling* Amma, do you know what this book is about?

Amma: *Chuckles* I know, ma. You have been asking me questions for months now. Do you think I don't see?

Me: *Laughs* You always see everything. But I don't think I've told you properly. It's about unlearning—the things we were told were normal but never felt right. It's about love, family, healing, and remembering what was taken from us.

Amma: *Nods slowly* Ah. So, you are doing what I have always done—telling stories so people don't forget.

Me: *Pauses, taken aback* I suppose I am. But you did it through your life, your words, your hands. I'm just writing it all down.

Amma: Writing is not *just* writing, ma. It is carrying forward what cannot be held in the hands. When I was young, we did not write down everything. We carried stories in our mouths, in our songs, in the way we lived. But now, the world moves too fast. If you do not write, who will remember?

Me: That's what I'm afraid of. That I won't do it justice. That I'll get it wrong.

Amma: *Shaking her head* You will not get it wrong, ma. You are writing from the heart. That is the only truth that matters.

A silence settles between us, warm and familiar. The sound of birds outside, the distant hum of a passing auto. She watches me, her eyes holding something deeper than words.

Me: Amma, when you look back… do you think we lost too much?

Amma: *Sighs* We lost, yes. But we also carried. When they told us how to love, we still found ways to hold each other. We are still here, aren't we?

Me: *Softly* We are.

Amma: *Smiles* And now, you are here, writing it all down. That is not loss, ma. That is victory.

Me: *Looking at her, heart full.* What do you want me to end the book with, Amma? What do you want the last words to be?

She closes her eyes for a moment, as if listening to something beyond us. Then she opens them, clear and steady.

Amma: End it with a promise. That we will remember. That we will not be ashamed of who we are. That love will not be a cage but a path. Tell them to hold each other. Tell them that nothing is truly lost if we choose to remember.

Me: *Whispers* I promise.

Introducing House of Hibiscus

Before I take you deeper into the work we do, I want to pause and tell you why it matters. Too often, mental health is spoken about in abstractions—clinical, distant, or overly polished. But what we've been building at Hibiscus is rooted in something far messier and more human: lived experience, collective care, and systemic change.

I'm explaining what we do not just to showcase our impact, but to offer a glimpse into what's *possible* when healing is made communal. Hibiscus is my life's work in motion—shaped by grief, resilience, laughter, and the belief that no one should ever feel alone in their suffering. This brief chapter isn't a brochure—it's a window into a dream we're living out, one conversation, one story, one act of care at a time.

Born out of lived experience and a deep desire to reimagine what healing could look like, *House of Hibiscus* is more than just an initative—it is a movement. It began with a simple belief: that mental health, justice, and dignity are not luxuries, but necessities for every human being.

What started as one woman's dream has grown into a collective force driven by youth, by women, by people who have known what it means to be silenced, dismissed, or forgotten. Under this umbrella, we built three bodies of work—each one distinct, but bound by a shared heartbeat: compassion in action.

- **Hibiscus Foundation for Social Welfare** began our journey in 2020, standing firmly for mental health, gender equity, climate action, and human rights. From conducting ground-level workshops in rural Tamil Nadu to creating national platforms for youth leadership, the Foundation has reached thousands.
- **Hibiscus Counselling**, our for-profit arm, was born in 2022 to provide affordable and deeply empathetic therapy services. Our team has supported thousands of clients, working with individuals, couples, and organizations to normalize and destigmatize emotional wellbeing.
- In 2024, we launched **Hibiscus Connect**, a digital tool for mental health professionals, helping therapists streamline their work while staying rooted in ethical, accessible practice.

Across it all, we've built spaces for people to feel seen—whether it's survivors of violence, children navigating disability, young adults facing burnout, or therapists learning to care for themselves too. From old age homes to IIT campuses, from urban clinics to remote districts, House of Hibiscus has made its way into lives that needed listening, not fixing.

So far, our impact has touched **over 2,00,000 individuals**, conducted **500+ workshops** and provided over **5000+ hours of therapy**. We run a community with over 5,000 Mental Health Professionals. But numbers alone can't capture what we've built. The real impact lies in the stories—the child who learned that anger isn't shameful, the couple who found their way back to each other, the therapist who realized they didn't have to carry it all alone.

The House of Hibiscus is rooted in Tamil soil, but our dreams reach far beyond. This is not just an organization. It is a rebellion against silence. A quiet revolution in care.

And we are just getting started.

Those Who Held Me

This book was never written alone. It carries the imprints of many hands, hearts, and histories.

To my husband, **Rajkumar Karunambigai Ramu,** thank you for being my steadfast companion and for holding space for this book to unfold.

To my dear friend **Fazil Razak,** for coining the word *Adaiyalam* and gifting this book its name—a word that holds so many layers of meaning, identity, and reclamation.

To **Indulekha** and **Kavya Datla,** whose friendship and feedback were foundational to shaping these chapters—thank you for reading with tenderness, patience, and fierce love.

To **Anandhi Akilan, Kalaibagyam, Ramu,** and **Iniya Mulai**—thank you for sharing your photographs, memories, and eyes through which I could see history differently.

To **Roshini Venkatesh,** who gave this book its face—thank you for designing a cover that held its spirit with such care.

To **Ramkrishnun Natrajhen,** for capturing me in the light I wanted to be seen—your photograph on the back cover holds more than an image; it holds a piece of this journey.

To my mother, for unearthing proverbs and sayings in Tamil that carried centuries of wisdom, and to my father, **Dr. Akilan Ramnathan**, for his quiet and unwavering guidance—thank you both for being my roots.

To my **ancestors**, known and unnamed, whose strength pulses through every page—this book is also yours.

To everyone else who held this process in invisible ways, and to those who will read it and carry it forward in your own journeys—I thank you.

To every single person who has worked with **Hibiscus Foundation for Social Welfare**, **Hibiscus Counselling**, and **Hibiscus Connect**—your labor, belief, and passion made this possible. This book is as much yours as it is mine.

And, finally, to those who stayed till the end

If you're holding this final page, I want to say something simple, and from the deepest part of me: thank you.

Writing this book wasn't easy. Not just because the stories were tender or the systems were complex—but because, for most of my life, *reading* itself has been hard. As someone with dyslexia, letters have often danced where I wanted them still. Words have overwhelmed me before they comforted me. Books, while beautiful, have never felt like the most welcoming place. And yet—I wrote one.

So if you picked up this book, supported this cause, and made it all the way through these pages, know this: I don't take your time or your effort lightly. I know what it means to *finish* something like this. I know the attention it demands, and I am grateful beyond words that you chose to give that attention to this work.

To be a dyslexic author is not just about overcoming difficulty. It's about redefining who gets to tell stories—and how they're told. It's about making space for voices that sound like mine, and maybe like yours too. This book is not perfect. But it is true. And it exists because people like you believe in what we're building together.

Thank you for reading. For feeling. For witnessing.

With all my heart,
Aksheyaa Akilan